THE
BEST
AMERICAN
POETRY
1990

◇ ◇ ◇

OTHER VOLUMES IN THIS SERIES

John Ashbery, editor *The Best American Poetry 1988*

Donald Hall, editor *The Best American Poetry 1989*

THE
BEST
AMERICAN
POETRY
1990

◇ ◇ ◇

Jorie Graham, Editor

David Lehman, Series Editor

COLLIER BOOKS

MACMILLAN PUBLISHING COMPANY

NEW YORK

COLLIER MACMILLAN CANADA

TORONTO

MAXWELL MACMILLAN INTERNATIONAL

NEW YORK • OXFORD • SINGAPORE • SYDNEY

Collier Books
Macmillan Publishing Company
866 Third Avenue, New York, N.Y. 10022

Collier Macmillan Canada, Inc.
1200 Eglinton Avenue East, Suite 200
Don Mills, Ontario M3C 3N1

ISBN 0-02-032785-4
ISSN 0-1040-5763

Macmillan books are available at special discounts for bulk purchases
for sales promotions, premiums, fund-raising, or educational use.
For details, contact:
Special Sales Director
Macmillan Publishing Company
866 Third Avenue
New York, N.Y. 10022

First Collier Books Edition 1990
10 9 8 7 6 5 4 3 2 1

Printed in the United States of America

CONTENTS

DAVID LEHMAN was born in New York City in 1948. His books include two poetry collections, *An Alternative to Speech* (1986) and *Operation Memory* (1990), both from Princeton University Press. His study of detective novels, *The Perfect Murder* (The Free Press, 1989), was nominated for an Edgar Award from the Mystery Writers of America. He is the editor of *Ecstatic Occasions, Expedient Forms: 65 Leading Contemporary Poets Select and Comment on Their Poems* (Collier Books, 1988). A Guggenheim Fellow in poetry for 1989–90, he lives with his wife and son in Ithaca, New York.

FOREWORD

by David Lehman

◊ ◊ ◊

The Best American Poetry, now in its third year, has already gone far to debunk some popular misconceptions. Poetry doesn't sell—yet the 1989 volume appeared last fall on a best-seller list compiled from independent bookstores. Poets are supposed to be the only audience poets can count on having—yet *The Best American Poetry* has been thoughtfully and generously reviewed by critics who do not themselves write poetry. The many positive responses to this series have helped to prove a point and to challenge a glib supposition. Poetry in the United States today does have a vital readership; rumors regarding the death of the reader have been greatly exaggerated.

Contemporary American poetry is said to be rife with sectarianism, though this book stands as evidence that the poets of rival sects may consort to their mutual enhancement. *The Best American Poetry* can't negotiate a truce among all the movements and schools and modes of writing poetry—there are simply too many of them, and the competitive impulse is as natural in an artist as in an athlete. But we can try to glean the best work being done today, irrespective of the biases of this man's region and that woman's literary allegiances. We can try to promote a more magnanimous spirit of response to the genuine article, wherever it may be found.

The rules of this anthology series are flexible and few. Each January a different guest editor, a poet of distinguished stature, makes the selections based on works published in the previous calendar year. No volume in the series will have fewer than fifty poems or more than seventy-five; there is a limit of three poems by an individual poet in any given year. The series editor is expected to support and assist the guest editor, in part by scanning magazines and making preliminary recommendations. Translations are ineligible, but there are otherwise no restrictions as to the form, the shape, and the style of the poems considered for inclusion.

I asked Jorie Graham to serve as this year's guest editor for several reasons—chief among them my admiration for her work. Though I could not prevail upon her to include a poem of her own in this volume, I was fascinated from start to finish by her profoundly ecumenical taste and could only marvel at her energy. It was clear to both of us that no two readers can realistically expect to keep up with all the poetry that is published in any given year. But we did our best—and the telephone company's records attest to our zeal for the project. Toward the end of the year, not a week went by without three or four long phone conversations during which fresh discoveries were read aloud and notes were compared on a new batch of periodicals. Nearly three dozen magazines are represented in *The Best American Poetry 1990*. We found our poems in *The New Yorker*, *The Atlantic*, and *The New Republic*; in campus quarterlies from Yale and Utah, Virginia and Denver, the University of the South and SMU; in *Antæus*, *Ploughshares*, and other sturdy mavericks; and in the numerous magazines with the singular names, *How(ever)*, *Fine Madness*, *Hanging Loose*, *O.blek*, *Avec*, and *Hambone*.

Jorie Graham is on the permanent faculty of the University of Iowa's Writers' Workshop, the oldest and arguably the most prestigious writing program in the country. To many, Iowa is regarded as the very heartland of creative writing—against which some polemicists have railed. We read about the "workshop" poem, the "perishable" poem that "didn't need to be written," the "safe" exercise in a fashionable idiom. This volume helps demolish that stereotype. Some of the most genuinely innovative poets in *The Best American Poetry 1990* attended creative writing programs at one time or another. At their best, it would seem, such programs offer young writers an extended parenthesis in their lives—a time to *live* poetry, if they wish, before they return to the diaspora of the working world.

In the pages that follow, the reader will encounter a plentiful amount of prose poetry, a pair of eclogues, "an old-fashioned song" and a sequence of "hermetic" ones, elegies, narratives, some fiercely religious lyrics, and several works that elevate punctuation marks to agents of poetic invention. The range of subject matter is broad, extending from Klaus Barbie to the Barbie doll; a meditation on Orpheus may segue into a telephone dialogue between a mother and son, to be followed in turn by the verbal encounter of "Aurora Borealis and the Body Louse." The variety of styles on display in this book is striking—and should combat the negative press that experimentalism too often receives. A number of the poems opt for unusual, seemingly improvised formal arrangements. Far from gratuitous, this emphasis on play seems bound up with a restless investigative spirit, and it helps give the poems their surface dazzle—they're as fresh as paint.

Our seventy-five contributors range from a college freshman to the current poet laureate of the United States. As in the previous volumes in the series, all were asked to comment on their poems, and many agreed to do so. The expansive section of contributors' notes in *The Best American Poetry* is intended not only to inform but to aid in fostering a direct relation between the reader and the voices behind the voices of the poems.

As this year's anthology headed into production, I wrote a poem to celebrate the completion of the book. The idea was to incorporate as many of the poets' names as possible, either directly or through homophones, echoes, and bilingual puns:

OUR REVELS

Walking along the strand, hand in hand,
We saw a cabin with the sign Lux et Veritas
Over the portal. The bearded man inside
Was eating graham crackers and reading Howards End.
A woman in Victorian garb bearing a dish of plums
Appeared out of nowhere. A bell tolled, sounding
Like the opening measures of Wagner's Flying Dutchman.

Down the hall (for the cabin was larger than it looked)
Children were speaking German. They exchanged little myths,

Wandering birds, magic mountains, and morning stars,
While the berry king, looking for an ash tray,
Announced that our revels were still in progress.
Then he quoted the divine opening of St. John's Gospel.
Love was the lever that lifted us above the amen corner.

We felt rich. And when we looked out the window,
We saw the spires of a medieval university
And Sherlock Holmes shadowing Professor Moriarty
Across a misty meadow. One hill, one man;
One gardener, one strip of galvanized steel;
One loaded shotgun, one moss-gathering stone;
A mill, a mule, a pin, a palm, a wading bather, a music stand.

And how would we know what to write
When we returned to our warren of offices
And gave up trying to keep up with the Joneses
And their kin, melting with ruth as we carved their names
On Birnam Wood, on the outskirts of the estate?
Dubious but determined, we gave up there for here:
Merrily, merrily, we welcomed in the year.

Walt Whitman is the bewhiskered gent, and Emily Dickinson the bearer of ripe fruit, in the poem's first stanza. They are invoked as the tutelary figures of American poetry.

In the course of 1989, the Berlin Wall came down, and the leaders of the United States and the Soviet Union declared the Cold War over. Americans were exhilarated by the speed of political change in the nations of Eastern Europe. Few things can be as heartening as the spectacle of a totalitarian state yielding, however grudgingly, some of its power to a popular democratic movement. In Czechoslovakia a poet and playwright, Vaclav Havel, became a national hero for his part in the Civic Forum mass movement. Early in the year he spent four months in jail; by year's end he was the president of a nation suddenly liberated from its forty-one-year-old Communist regime. But 1989 was also a year in which a head of state called for the assassination of a prominent novelist; and for writers and publishers closer to home, it seemed a year of threats, overt or camouflaged, to their freedom of expression. A tyrannical edict, proposed though happily not executed, concentrates the mind wonderfully—it makes us realize how fragile a thing is a writer's liberty. How good it is to celebrate the freedom of the word, knowing that art still has the ability to inflame passions, disturb the complacent, and arouse the anxiety of despots.

JORIE GRAHAM was born in New York City in 1950. Raised in Italy by her American parents, she studied philosophy at the Sorbonne and filmmaking at New York University. She worked in television before she entered the Writers' Workshop at the University of Iowa, where she received her Master of Fine Arts. She has been awarded fellowships from the Guggenheim, Whiting, and Ingram Merrill foundations and from the National Endowment for the Arts. Her books of poetry include *Hybrids of Plants and of Ghosts* (Princeton University Press, 1980), *Erosion* (Princeton, 1983), and *The End of Beauty* (Ecco Press, 1987). A new collection, *Region of Unlikeness*, is forthcoming from Ecco. A professor of English at the University of Iowa, Jorie Graham lives with her husband and daughter in Iowa City.

INTRODUCTION

by Jorie Graham

◊ ◊ ◊

I

I went to a reading recently—fiction and poetry. It was a warm Indian summer night. The man introducing spoke first about the novelist—her meteoric rise to the top along the fast track. Book awards. Movie deals. The person in question stood up and read wonderful, funny stories. I laughed out loud; listened to the sentences flowing by—their aggressive overtaking of the space. There was no silence, there was the *run run* of story over it all. It sprayed forward over the unsaid until it was all plot. People changed or didn't. You felt at home.

Then our host introduced the poet—one of our very best. The introductory remarks referred to the "dark times poetry is in." People resettled in their chairs. The man in question stood up to read, looked out at us over his glasses, cleared his throat. He tried to say something funny to put us at our ease, but we weren't. What was he going to do? Where did the wonderful warm sensation of *story* go? A poem began. Not a little story told in musical rhythms, but a poem. Oh, it had story. And it was music. But it seemed to begin out of nowhere. And it moved irrationally—by the standards the fiction had set. It leapt. It went too suddenly to the heart of the matter. Why was I feeling so uneasy? I didn't feel myself thinking anymore. I wasn't feeling lifted or entertained. My hands felt heavy. My body felt heavy. The air into which language had been pouring for almost an hour felt heavy.

Then I started to hear it: the silence; the words chipping into the silence. It felt loud. Every word stood out. No longer the rush of sentences free and unresisted into the air. Now it was words cutting into an element that was crushing in its power and weight. I thought of Sartre's notion that prose writers tame language and that it's up to poetry to set it free again. I thought of the violence from within summoned up to counter the violence from without. I looked at the man and listened. His words cut into the unsaid and made me hear it: its depth and scope; its indifference, beauty, intractability.

Listening, I became aware of how much each poem resisted the very desires that the fiction, previously, had satisfied. Every word was clear, yes, every image clear—but the motion of the poem as a whole resisted my impulse to resolve it into "sense" of a rational kind. Listening to the poem, I could feel my irritable reaching after fact, my desire for resolution, graspable meaning, ownership. I *wanted* to narrow it. I wanted to make it into a shorter version of the other experience, the story. It resisted. It compelled me to let go. The frontal, grasping motion frustrated, my intuition was forced awake. I felt myself having to "listen" with other parts of my sensibility, felt my mind being forced back down into the soil of my senses. And I saw that it was the resistance of the poem—its occlusion, or difficulty—that was healing me, forcing me to privilege my heart, my intuition—parts of my sensibility infrequently called upon in my everyday experience in the marketplace of things and ideas. I found myself feeling, as the poem ended, that some crucial muscle that might have otherwise atrophied from lack of use had been exercised. Something part body, part spirit. Something the species should never evolve away from. Something I shouldn't be living without. *The poem must resist the intelligence / almost successfully*, whispered Wallace Stevens.

II

Yet surely the most frequent accusation leveled against contemporary poetry is its difficulty or inaccessibility. It is accused of speaking only to itself, or becoming an irrelevant and elitist art form with a dwindling audience. And indeed, contemporary poetry's real or apparent difficulty has made it seem somewhat like an intransigent outsider—or perhaps a high-minded purist—in the vast hungry field of American art. And this, in turn, affects how many poets conceive of their enterprise. For how often can we hear that "no one reads it," or that "no one understands it," without experiencing a failure of confidence, however inchoate? And how easily that failure of confidence converts to self-hatred, causing some of us to write articles about the death of poetry, or the horrors of creative writing programs, and others to turn on our own poems, prescribing rules, announcing remedies, saying narrative is all there is or should be, saying *self* should be ostracized, saying free verse is fatal, or all rhyme and meter reactionary, talking about elitism, about how poetry has failed to communicate to the common reader, until finally we cease to trust the power of poetry. We "accept the limitations" of the medium. We start believing that it is essentially anachronistic. We become anecdotal. We want to entertain. We believe we should "communicate" . . .

One problem might stem from the fact that poetry implicitly undertakes a critique of materialist values. It rests on the assumption that material values need to be seen through—or at least complicated sufficiently—in earnest or truer, or more resonant, more supple values. No doubt many of the attacks against poetry come from those of us who, uncomfortable with our slippery marriage to American materialism and its astounding arrogant excess, wish, however unconsciously, that poetry would avert its scrutiny. Or from those of us who turned to poetry at a more idealistic time in our lives and who now rage against it as we lose the capacity for idealism—dreamers turned insomniacs, accusing the dream of having failed them.

But, these basic issues aside, the difficulty of poetry, even for its most sympathetic readers, is a real one. Or rather it is both real and imagined. Much of it dissipates as one opens up to the experience of poetry. To comprehend poetry one must, after all, practice by reading it. As to "see" modern dance, one must at least know its vocabulary, its texture, what the choreographer chose *not* to do. As to understand good carpentry one must be able to grasp what the maker's options were, what the tradition is, what the nature of wood is, what the structural necessities were: what is underpinning, what flourish and passion, what *decor*. Of course, with woodworking or ballet, one can still enjoy what one barely grasps. And such pleasure would also be possible with poetry if intimidation didn't set in: intimidation created by its apparently close relation to the normal language of discourse; fear that one is missing the point or, worse, that one is stupid, blind.

Poetry can also be difficult, though, because much of it attempts to render aspects of experience that occur outside the provinces of logic and reason, outside the realm of narrative realism. The ways in which dreams proceed, or magic, or mystical vision, or memory, are often models for poetry's methods: what we remember upon waking, what we remember at birth—all the brilliant Irrational in the human sensibility. Poetry describes, enacts, is compelled by those moments of supreme passion, insight or knowledge that are physical yet intuitive, that render us whole, *inspired*. Among verbal events—which by their nature move horizontally, through time, along the lines of cause and effect—poetry tends to leap, to try to move more vertically: astonishment, rapture, vertigo—the seduction of the infinite and the abyss—what so much of it is after. "Ever more ancient and naked states" (Octavio Paz).

In fact, one could argue that poetry's difficulty for some readers stems from the very source of its incredible power: the merging of its irrational procedures with the rational nature of language. So that one mistake we often make is as simple as expecting poetry to be apprehended by the same reading methods and habits that "grasp" prose. While instead—mere practice and exposure to the art form aside—it's probably more a matter of avoiding the interference of fear in reading; more a matter of reading with one's most natural instincts and senses.

That's what is perhaps wrongheaded about the arguments often mounted today against poetry's alleged lack of accessibility to "ordinary" Americans. Aren't such accusations of elitism rather condescending to the people on whose behalf they are made? As if the non-literary men and women of America somehow didn't dream? As if associational logic were restricted to the educated? As if a portion of American readers were only able to read poems of narrative simplicity, having somehow—because of their work experience or background—lost all intuition and sensory intelligence? Isn't this line of thinking, in effect, another sympton of the distrust many of us feel regarding the very core of poetry, its inherent way of proceeding, its nature? I think of Umberto Eco in a recent radio interview: How do you explain that your books, so difficult, sell in the hundreds of thousands of copies in America? "Well," he replied, as if surprised by the question, "in my experience, people, ordinary people, like difficulty. They are tired of being treated like they can't get it. They want it. I give them what they want."

There is, however, another difficulty connected to the poetry of this historical (or posthistorical?) moment. It might be best understood as the result of poetry's confrontation with certain aspects of the culture—particularly its distrust of speech and of what is perceived as the terminal "slowness" of speech in relation to the speedier verbal image as a medium for sales (of objects, people, ideas, of verisimilitude, of desire).

As visual imagery largely supplants speech as the language of choice for most cultural transactions (since most constitute a form of sales), it brings with it, in its shadow, new (fin-de-siècle?) attitudes for poets to contend with: a pervasive distrust of *thinking* people; a distrust of rhetorical power (of articulate speech in general); a disrespect for all nonlucrative activities; a general impatience with depth, and a shortened attention span.

Sound bites, shortcuts, clips, trailers, minimalist fragmented "dialogue," the Reagan-era one-liner on the way to the helicopter: the speed with which an idea must be "put across" is said to be determined not just by monetary considerations, but by the speeded-up, almost decimated attention span of the bored, overstimulated viewer who must be caught, bought, on the wing, as he or she is clicking past, "grazing" the channels, wanting to be stopped, but only momentarily.

As a collective emotion this distrust of language is, of course, one that each of us is free to subvert, override. But precisely because it is a collective emotion, it is one that much poetry inevitably incorporates, explores or enacts as not only an anxiety concerning its very reason to exist, but also as an anxiety concerning the nature and function of language, its capacity for seizing and transmitting . . . *truth*? Even that word seems tinged with regret, nostalgia, in such an atmosphere.

For isn't the essential characteristic of speech, and the particular virtue of its slowness, that it permits the whole fabric to be *received* by a listener—idea, emotion, fact, product, plot detail, motive— the listener having enough *time* to make up his or her mind?

Isn't to describe, to articulate an argument, to use language at the speed where the complexity and sonorousness of syntax and cadence reach the listener, to use it so that the free will of the listener is addressed—free will it is the very purpose of salesmanship to bypass? The genius of syntax consists in its permitting paradoxical, "unsolvable" ideas to be *explored*, not merely nailed down, stored, and owned; in its permitting the soul-forging pleasures of thinking to prevail over the acquisition of information called knowing.

That this is an essential aspect of the activity of poetry as we know it seems obvious, yet in an atmosphere in which the very notion that a reader might grasp or "receive" the poem written by the writer is questioned, on the one hand, and in which the much of the audience wants to be zapped, fast, as it clicks down the dial on the other, the whole enterprise becomes, in many cases, fraught with anxiety.

And though these concerns have been present, to some extent, in the poetry of the English language for some time, it is the vehemence (and in some instances the desperation) with which they creep into the formal, aesthetic and thematic concerns of our poems (and into the very writing process)—the incredible tension between the desire to return to "slower" uses of language and the historical values they still transmit, and an equally strong desire to rebel against the very nature of language—its slowness, its referentiality—that most vividly characterizes American poetry as I encountered it in 1989.

III

Sometimes the distrust of language results in the refusal to use words denotatively. There are "language-events," for example, that imply a need to rely on other media in order to restore to language the depth or wholeness it seems to lack. As they can't be reproduced in an anthology such as this one, some examples might be of use.

A recent work by Leslie Scalapino, for example, whose "instructions" read: "done by four or five people as movements as if the words were music." Or the language-work done for the Margaret Jenkins Dance Company by a number of poets which is used as "music": a long liquid verbal text stretched out electronically, sometimes shattered, to make it suitable as a backdrop to dance. The newest "works" by Jenny Holzer consist of phrases and words (and it seems clear that almost any words will do) carved into granite, projected in neon.

Looking at other temperaments—and, more specifically, at some of the work represented in this anthology—we find a renewed fascination with very high diction, surfaces that call attention to themselves as unnatural in relation to ordinary human speech. This highly self-conscious use of language points fiercely to our distrust of the natural, the spoken—as if to insist that for us, now, the beautiful (the true?) is not in nature but in artifice. It points as well, to the problem of subjectivity and the active struggle with Romantic and Modernist notions of *reality* and the *self* that so many of these poems enact.

Our so-called Language Poets take a different tack. In their work we often see the dismantling of articulate speech in an effort to recover a *prior* version of self, a cleaner one, free of cultural association—a language free of its user! In this volume numerous poems work toward the forcible undoing of the sentence, but they also explore for us the notion of *right choice* in diction, and the whole relationship of choice of word to *choice* in its broadest sense. In some of the more radical work, the word is privileged over the phrase and the sentence. One can see this as a corrective measure against the political and cultural excesses the sentence is a metaphor for; one can see it, too, as an attempt to redefine the nature of sense itself. In fact in such poems meaning itself is often questioned as a cultural value, and chance and the inner laws of language are asked to reign as tutelary deities. In them, too, the silence is argued with most excitingly: a silence at times loud and deeply empowered, at times violently reduced to mere white space on a page.

Then there are those who fall, perhaps, under the heading of narrative poets. In them we see a passionate determination to re-claim the power of articulate speech via its more "traditional" methods: plot, cause and effect, the spun web of storytelling. These poems often refuse the swift association, deep economy, leaping of mind, and structural use of analogy which many of the "pure" lyric poets favor. It is as if these more strictly lyric methods were seen as being, in some manner, partially responsible for the breakdown of speech's powers: the holes they allow in the fabric of telling seen as having finally gotten too big, the net no longer able to hold the mystery, the swift prey.

The ambition to reclaim ground for eloquence and rhetoric is perhaps even more starkly visible in the sharp, urgent poems of sheer argument—the lyric-essay, which seems to be flourishing, stark offspring of the more classic meditation, also in vogue.

One important formal development is the recent popularity of prose poems. We might think of them as, perhaps, the frontal approach; they are certainly—in many cases—the most extreme in their attempt to use the strategies of "normal" articulate speech to reach the reader. Their number, variety and sheer quality (and the extraordinarily different uses to which the form is put) caused me to think of this volume as, in part, a subterranean exploration of the form.

Yet another battle fought over the power and nature of articulate speech predates our current anxieties. For when we get to the work of some of our so-called minimalists, we are faced with a more historical (and American) distrust of articulateness: "inarticulateness" as stoicism, perhaps—the terseness we recognize in our Western folk heroes—as if to speak a full sentence, to yield to easeful speech, were a sensual activity one cannot, or should not, afford to indulge.

This is verbal reticence of a vastly different order from that caused by the fear or distrust described above. Rather, it is better seen as a metaphysical condition in which language is fully mastered but withheld. It dovetails, in some instances, with the symbolist sense of the alchemical power of each word, or Zen notions of restraint, or the objectivist desire to honor the resistance of the material world and attempt a suppression of ego—(George Oppen: "It is necessary to be afraid of words, it is necessary to be afraid of each word, every word").

In most instances this distrust of eloquence is sinewed by the desire for sincerity. The longing for the "pure clear word," to use James Wright's phrase, expresses a deeply-held American belief that the simpler the utterance—the closer to the bone of the feeling—the better the chance of getting the *self* through uncontaminated by language: speech a vehicle that can "betray" honest feeling when it becomes too ornate or "articulate"; the self imagined as existing in some form prior to speech, *inside*, forced to translate itself out (a passage that can betray the "pure" self, can misshape, lie).

If we look at the Puritan conviction (still alive as a "law" among the Amish) that to use more words than required—more than the absolute minimum to get the thing said—is sinful, we can feel the dimensions of this belief. The Amish to this day can be shunned for such garrulousness—it being relegated to the level of promiscuity.

There is, however, another version of selfhood: Elizabethan, dramatic, created in performance, created precisely *by* acts of speech. It involves a whole other set of assumptions about the location and nature of selfhood—assumptions both more "primitive" (as in many native ritualistic dramatic ceremonies by which the self is "invented" or "invoked") and more "sophisticated" (the Language Poets, for example, share the notion of a constructed self—although they tend to regard it with suspicion).

At any rate the notion of a *mask* or mythic persona created by language competes with the tradition of "honest" speech on American soil, and there are many poets (this reader would argue that it is all the significant ones) who attempt to merge the two impulses: in most instances they marry, apparently happily, and the struggle goes underground; in some the tension between the two is carried out on the surface of the poem.

For others, minimalism of phrasing—or more precisely, decimated, sputtered phrasing—is not a question of reticence or stoicism. Rather, it is a mixture of inward abbreviation and the kind of speediness imposed on the language of someone who wishes to be heard (or to hear himself) above an assembly line. Phrasing fragmented as much by competition with the machine (whose purpose it is to silence the spirit?) as by mental exhaustion. There is an element in it, too, of the coding covert political activity requires.

In yet others, the fragmentation of phrasing would seem to be occasioned by the speaker's encounter with something *in* the silence that is spiritually overwhelming. One is reminded of Emily Dickinson's "I know that He exists / Somewhere—in silence."

Ultimately, how one extends outward into the silence—narratively, metrically, in fragments, in prose—involves the nature of how that silence is perceived. For it is the desire to engage the silence, and the resistance of that silence, that tugs at speech; silence the field into which the voice, the mind, the heart play out their drama. One cannot run out to play when the field has been replaced by a void. One stays away or walks back and forth at the edge of that void. Sometimes imagining where the field had *been* works for a while. But more likely one will give up, go home. As the field of genuine silence thins or vanishes for many of us—or is replaced with *noise*—an interesting thing starts to happen. We hear it most dramatically in the work of many of our youngest poets: the voice is raised; anger, rage, parodic manic energy, irony, violence, push back at the noise to create a space to live in, to think and feel in, the violence from within more violent than ever before perhaps because the violence from without, against which it pushes, is so great.

For some poets the poem is a critique of the powers of representation, so they seem more concerned with the possibility of saying something than with what is said. Such poems present themselves as investigations rather than as conclusions. Words—or the gaps between them—are used to recompose a world, as if these poets were looking for a method by which to *experience* the world once again. We might find ourselves being asked implicitly where the poem actually *is*: In the world? In the language? In the reader's interpretation or in the poet's intention? Or does it float somewhere between—and is that *somewhere between* chance or fate? The only thing we are left with, perhaps, the only bedrock, is the writer's commitment to writing. Notes, letters, journals, findings, memory patches, neo-impressionist accumulations, a distrust of direct statement and direct apprehension; the moral issue becomes, Can anyone trust the world enough to *write it down*?

When we experience a loosening of setting or point of view, and a breakdown of syntax's dependence on closure, we witness an opening up of the present-tense terrain of the poem, a privileging of delay and digression over progress.

This opening up of the present moment as a terrain outside time—this foregrounding of the field of the "act of the poem"— can be explained in many ways. We might consider the way in which the idea of *perfection* in art seems to be called into question by many of our poets. On the one hand, some might argue today, the notion of perfection serves ultimately to make an object not so much ideal as available to a marketplace, available for ownership —something to be acquired by the act of understanding.

Perhaps more important, the notion of "conjuring up a form with words that resists the action of time" (to use Zbigniew Herbert's phrase) is put into question by the poetics of many of these poets (most radically by the "language" poets, but also by many others—the writers of prose poems, the poets who break their lines forcibly against syntax, the increasingly elliptical lyric poets) because the figures for a timeless, or eternal, realm we can summon up most readily are the nuclear winter, the half-life of radioactive waste, and extinctions of various kinds. Not "eternities" we would, or could, want our poems to exist in. Not the kind we would want to transcend time to inhabit.

A number of the poems in this book—and many others I admired but couldn't include—are longer than average. Perhaps in order to make themselves felt as the *field of action*, in order to bring to life, via digression and delay, a realm outside the linear and ending-dependent motions of history, narrative, progress, manifest destiny, upward mobility. Their length insures that the motion toward closure will be itself part of the subject. Will it be fought? Will it be earned? Much of the work here that uses of serial (i.e., constantly re-beginning) structures is looking for a sense of form that is not so ending-dependent. It asks, in other words, if perhaps we can no longer afford for Death to be the only mother of Beauty. . . .

Finally, many of these works use devices that break the fluid progress of the poem, that destabilize the reader's relationship to the illusion of the poem as text spoken by a single speaker in deep thought, aroused contemplation, or recollection. These interferences force the reader out of a passive role and back into the poem as an active participant. I do not, by any means, intend that the reader become what is sometimes called the "co-creator" of the text. Rather, what I admire in these poems is the controlled way each poet has found to coax the reader into a new—shall we say *awakened?*—state without handing over the reins of the poem either to pure *chance* or to that embodiment of chance, the bored, barely willing, barely attentive, overstimulated (i.e., shut down) reader.

Indeed, one could argue that the poems in this collection that do not let us become comfortable with plot, point of view, setting, eventually force us to read in a different way; force us to let music take the place of narrative flow; force us to let our senses do some of the work we would "normally" be letting our conscious minds do. We discover, in the process, that we can trust a deeper current of our sensibility, something other than the lust-for-forwardness, with all its attendant desires for closure, shapeliness, and the sense that we are *headed somewhere* and that we are in the *hands of something*. We are forced to suspend these desires, to let the longing stay alive unsatisfied; forced to accord power to a portion of ourselves and a portion of the world we normally deem powerless or feminine or "merely" intuitive.

And then, lastly, throughout this volume, you'll find the undiminished, or unintimidated, eloquence of our classical believers— perhaps only apparently unperturbed by the desperate fray; poets in whom the repose of counted language is perhaps the highest form, today, of bravery.

IV

What is especially interesting about poetry's current situation is that it is practically alone, among the art forms being practiced, in still viewing the artist as essentially an outsider to the marketplace. And perhaps there is reason to celebrate that this Romantic-Modernist vision is, for the most part, given the economic limits of the life of the poet, still a reality. It's ultimately due to the very nature of the enterprise. "Where," said the teacher, ripping the page containing Keats' poem out of the book, crumpling it up and tossing it into the waste can across the room, "where is the *Ode on a Grecian Urn* now?" . . .

The particular advantage of this position for the poet is that it makes poetry's task as a moral and spiritual undertaking more starkly clear than ever. And the renewed fascination—on all sides of the aesthetic spectrum—with formal techniques that foreground process, indicates the rediscovery, by yet another generation of poets, of the ways in which the act of the poem is identical with a spiritual questing. A rediscovery of the ways in which the honing of one's tools for *sight*—formal techniques—*is* the honing of one's tools for *insight*.

After all, great poems are language acts of amazing precision, acts in which precision is coincident with humility. The human sensibility, via language, moves to its object of scrutiny and gives way to it, letting it stain the language. The imagination goes out as far as it can into the thing and comes back imprinted. One of the great mysteries in poetry centers on the way in which the crisp and honest description of the outer world schools one for the encounter with one's inner reality. To see clearly is to think clearly: a commonplace. To see clearly and think clearly is to feel deeply: a mystery.

The poetry that fails the genius of its medium today is the poetry of mere self. It embarrasses all of us. The voice in it not large but inflated. A voice that expands not to the size of a soul (capable of being both personal and communal, both private and historical) but to the size of an ego. What I find most consistently moving about the act of a true poem is the way it puts the self at genuine risk. The kind of risk Robert Frost refers to when he describes the "ideals of form" as "where all our ingenuity is lavished on getting into danger legitimately so that we may be genuinely rescued."

To place oneself at genuine risk, that the salvation effected be genuine (i.e., of use to us), the poet must move to encounter an other, not more versions of the self. An other: God, nature, a beloved, an Idea, Abstract form, Language itself as a field, Chance, Death, Consciousness, what exists in the silence. Something not invented by the writer. Something the writer risks being defeated—or silenced—by. A poem is true if it can effect that encounter. All matters of style, form, and technique refer to that end.

That is why precision is so crucial: on it depends the nature of the encounter; on it depends whether the poet achieves or fails at the discovery. That is what Pound means, I believe, by his famous formula describing technique as a measure of the poet's sincerity. How sincere are we about wanting to go where the act of a poem might take us? Do we not often, instead, take the poem merely where *we* want to go—protecting ourselves. . . . In the end how sincere we truly are, how desperate and committed we are, is revealed by how hard we are on ourselves, how sharp we are willing to make our instruments.

So that, for this reader of the poetry of 1989, precision remained the watershed criterion. A poem, however difficult in its overall strategy, needs to be, step by step, precise, accurate, clear. Where the senses are used in language, the image needs to be seized, not approximated. Where the mind moves abstractly in language to grasp, outline, blurt into an idea, it does so with precision. Vague thinking, blurry emotion, approximate sensation—and their slippery cousins, sentimental, "poetic" sensation—are not, I hope, what we mean by difficulty in poetry. They are failures of encounter, failures of perception, failures of character even. Difficulty is a powerful tool and not in any way synonymous with imprecision, laziness, lack of descriptive power.

The bedrock role of poetry, ultimately, is to restore, for each generation anew, the mind to its word and the words to their world via accurate usage. Every generation of poets has that task, and it must—each time—do it essentially from scratch. Each image achieved, each moment of description where the *other* is seized, where it stains the language, undertakes that same vast metaphysical work: to restore the human *word* to the immortal thing; to insure that the relationship is, however momentarily, viable and true. Free of decor. Free of usury, exaggeration. To make the words channels between mind and world. To make them *full* again.

Each poem is, in the end, an act of the mind that tries—via precision of seeing, feeling, and thinking—to clean the language of its current lies, to make it capable of connecting us to the world, to the *there*, to insure that there be a *there* there. For it is when we convince ourselves that it is not really wholly there—the world, the text, the author's text, the intention—that we are free, by the mere blinking of a deconstructing eye, to permit its destruction. It can't be *taken* from us if it's not there. It's up to language to make sure that it *is* there, and so much there, that its loss would not be an act of interpretation—a sleight of hand—but an act of murder.

V

As for what is *American* about these poems. . . . There is what I consider a totally American moment at the end of the movie *A Life Lived* about the painter Philip Guston. He sits before what had been a very large, very complex, completed painting. We had been "watching" him paint it, on and off, throughout the movie. Now it has been totally whitewashed and erased. It had been very strong. *What happened*, the interviewer asks. Well, the artist replies, yes, it did get done, and it was, yes, a good one. But it was too good. It was a *painting painting*, he says. And besides, it happened too fast. I didn't have the experience, he says. I don't want the painting without the experience. It happened too fast.

Much of the poetry I read this year was trying both to *happen fast* and *have the experience*. That is the signature ambition of our current poetry, what is so brave in it, so American.

Another way to say this is that our poems promote *voice*—and personality—but not at the expense of form and not at the expense of imagery. They jazz the surface up—they let themselves be seen through—they ham it up, they are totally, tragically aware of themselves as surfaces, as media events, as punctured through with temporality (the minutes click by loudly in them as if paid for at advertiser's rates), and yet they still insist on the deep song, the undertow, the classical griefs and celebrations. They try to be both deeply historical and utterly ahistorical—breakdancing on the surface and breaking the flow of anything that would thicken into *history*. They are, in other words, both in history and somehow beyond it: the American moment: still in the story we've told ourselves of ourselves, still wanting that weight to slow us down, that sense of manifest destiny, of progress—and yet tragically outside it, playing the part out, crackling on the surface in that dizzy, irreverent self-knowledge that passes today for freedom. A more tragic predicament is hard to imagine. That we are making art out of such being-seen-through; that we—the estuary through which the past is suddenly thrust into the vast cold currents of total self-consciousness, capitalism's furthermost chapter—are making song out of such a predicament is amazing and very moving to this witness.

VI

Finally, although the diversity of the work is staggering, and reminds one of how truly huge this nation is—how many different kinds of experience it affords us by its very expanse and variety of landscape—I still found it impossible to generalize about origins when it came to the strong work. Urban poetry did not own certain poetic procedures. The most "radical" poems in the anthology come from poets in Arizona, Washington, North Carolina, New York City, Massachusetts, Iowa, California—from graduates of writing programs, from graduates of factories, offices, happy childhoods, miserable childhoods. The metrical verse is equally widely distributed as to geographic origin and personal background. I found no voice exclusively attached to region, race, gender, class; no concerns limited by region, race, gender, and class. And I found very few "pure" examples of one or another aesthetic camp—finding many more poems to be incredibly fruitful and moving hybrids of styles, techniques and aesthetic premises. I wouldn't like to call on the notion of postmodern style to explain the kind of hybridization I found, because the tone in which these marriages of technique are undertaken is rarely ironic. Instead it seems to me that the very seriousness of the stylistic searching going on here—and the degree to which the poems increasingly enact a deep spiritual longing—speaks to a genuine revival of poetic ambition. The poetic map of the country reads far less like a set of rival encampments, as the various polemicists would have us believe, and far more like a wonderfully varied and passionate family argument, in which much cross-pollination is going on. Excitement and the spirit of birthing far override the contentious spirit of analysis and prescription.

In the end, all these poems seem deeply political to me. Some explicitly, some implicitly. They all speak about the condition of the Republic. As for the matter of overt communication—as in the frequently asked question, *Who is the audience for these poems?*—the poet speaks from the condition of his time. He doesn't address his fellows, he speaks in their behalf. He is their voice. This is how we sound. Whether or not we listen to ourselves is less important than whether we raise our voice to speak, whether we raise it with courage, skill and integrity, or whether we flounder in inaccuracy. These poets are hard on themselves, their skill is immense, they believe in hard work (that it will produce truth), and they speak for us.

THE
BEST
AMERICAN
POETRY
1990

◇ ◇ ◇

The Damned

◇ ◇ ◇

This fellow grazed his woolly goats
on a high ledge, a very high place
snowless in summer, but it was,

perhaps because of the fellow's loneliness,
a region in which the mountains talked,
it seemed, and over a miles-wide gulf,

summits forever white rose useless
in august assumptions the polish of
the wind and glare of the sun sanctified,

the fellow supposed, and he thought,
well, few know that kind of thing,
a rare condition, though not good for grass:

and the fellow, noting that the peaks
had really said nothing yet, went to
the ledge-edge and looked down on the

summits of sweet-green hills
and runoff rills so lowly and supposed,
again, that these damned came of being

near the sanctified, wherever one finds
one one finds the other, and he wondered
if the heights knew, somehow, that the energy

of their complacency came of
a differentiation imposed on the backs,
so to speak, of the lowly, and he

wondered if the sanctified would not
wish to remove themselves, somehow, if
they knew that, but then, he supposed,

knowing that would spoil the sanctification
anyhow, so maybe the peaks could shine
there, since it seemed they had to, as

wastelands of what it means to be way high:
but the mountains had said nothing and
the fellow supposed himself a supposition,

too, no one having agreed with him, the peaks
too taken aback, except for this longing
for the valleys roaring in his guts.

from *The Yale Review*

The Sweeping Gesture

◇ ◇ ◇

in the sky was final above
the hospital that was the color of bread.
The pigeons cooed and made a home
under the fire-escape. Emptiness

like a permanent echo
remained in the streets, although the ghosts
of punks and panhandlers hovered
in the improvised bazaars,
stepping between photographs of limbs
splayed and bronzed, or torsos
uniformly "god-like" in repose.

Another classic scene. The question arose:
"If the people in the city dress as if
for the beach, what do they wear at the beach?
What pleasure is there in continual
freedom from restraints?" The grid
is dropped over all colors and complaints,
and assigns to each its portion and locale.
The wind lifts the trash a little way to where
the sun sears the rose leaves, and a hand
reaches for the warm drink that was cool
a moment ago. —O air,
for some weeks absent from these shores! . . .

It is too early to leave and far beyond the point
when departure would have made a difference. You
sigh at this but continue packing anyway:

"On the island there are trees, and above them
are houses open to the slightest movement of the air,
and red-winged birds come to rest
on the weathered railings of their decks; under
the trees tunnels run from the ocean to the bay,
and all day we see what comes and goes away.
Only, over Babylon, a dull cloud hangs."

So much for letters home
(the kind that are never sent).
There must be more to it than heaven or hell,
our dirt and their purity, something
that could stand contradiction
without collapsing in a frenzy,
but you are already more cool and distant
than a waterfall: you were never here,
never belonged in these streets and avenues
when a single tree's survival seems
a miracle,—and they are here
in thousands, the planes, the honey-locusts,
veiling the high cornices of rusticated
tenements, the smiling capitals of wealthy houses.

All the other places that come to mind
(possible locations of other lives
that might have been ours with a change of luck)
are neither exotic nor blessed:
they too are a part of what we call *home*,—
towers and bridges, wild flowers, boulevards,
mountains and demolished smokestacks,
and however far away the singer may be
the song still arrives with news from the hotel
of the red quilt a mother stitched with stars.

It is time for these things to be part of understanding,
for mere opinion and impotent rage to diminish
to a murmur, a background harmony like the sob
of an off-stage horn, time for the art of illumination
to be revived in golden air. Already the small, blue
ferryboat puts out from the dock towards home or the city.

Minutes of silence are observed with every dawn
and the buildings grow taller with news of each loss.

from *Broadway*

Notes from the Air

◊ ◊ ◊

A yak is a prehistoric cabbage: of that, at least, we may be sure.
But tell us, sages of the solarium, why is that light
still hidden back there, among houseplants and rubber sponges?
For surely the blessed moment arrived at midday

And now in midafternoon lamps are lit,
for it is late in the season. And as it struggles now
and is ground down into day, complaints
are voiced at the edges of darkness: Look, it says,

it has to be this way and no other. Time that one seizes
and takes along with one is running through the holes
like sand from a bag. And these sandy moments
accuse us, are just what our enemy ordered,

the surly one on his throne of impacted
gold. No matter if our tale be interesting
or not, whether children stop to listen and through the rent
veil of the air the immortal whistle is heard,

and screeches, songs not meant to be listened to.
It was some stranger's casual words, overheard in the windblown
street, above the roar of the traffic and then swept
to the distant orbit where words hover: *Alone*, it says,

but you slept. And now everything is being redeemed,
even the square of barren grass that adjoins your doorstep,
too near for you to see. But others, children and others, will
when the right time comes. Meanwhile we mingle, and not

because we have to, because some host or hostess
has suggested it, beyond the limits of polite
conversation. And we, they too, were conscious of having
known it, written on the flyleaf of a book presented as a gift

at Christmas 1882. No more trivia, please, but music
in all the spheres leading up to where the master
wants to talk to you, place his mouth over yours,
withdraw that human fishhook from the crystalline flesh

where it was melting, give you back your clothes, penknife,
twine. And where shall we go when we leave? What tree is bigger
than night that surrounds us, is full of more things,
fewer paths for the eye and fingers of frost for the mind,

fruits halved for our despairing instruction, winds
to suck us up? If only the boiler hadn't exploded one
could summon them, icicles out of the rain, chairs enough
for everyone to be seated in time for the lesson to begin.

from *The New Yorker*

Victim of Himself

◇ ◇ ◇

He thought he saw a long way off the ocean
cresting and falling, bridging the continents,
carrying the whole sound of human laughter
and moans—especially moans, in the mud of misery—
but what he saw was already diluted, evaporating,
and what he felt were his teeth grinding
and the bubbles of saliva that broke on his tongue.

He was doomed to be a victim of himself.
He thought he saw, in the future, numberless, cavernous
burials—the outcome of plagues, of wars,
of natural disasters created by human beings—
but what he saw was already faded, disintegrating,
and what he felt was the normal weakness displayed
by droopy eyes and muscles that bleated meekly.

He thought he saw from Earth up to the stars
and from any one moment back to the hour of his birth
when desire produced, in the slush of passionate tides,
a citizen of mud and ash, of lost light and dry beds,
but what he saw was already distorted, moving away,
and what he felt was a sense of loss that so often
he had been at peace in her arms when he did not intend to be.

from *The Atlantic Monthly*

First Song / Bankei / 1653 /

◇   ◇   ◇

never was   always will be
mind before mind
earth water fire wind
sleep there tonight

you you on fire
burning yourself
attached
to this burning house

search
all the way back
to the womb
can't remember a thing

good bad
ideas
self self
which?

winter's wonderful
bonfire's
ridiculous
in summer

summer breezes
irritate
even before autumn's
over

rich now
you hate the poor
forget when you
had nothing

you saved every dollar
a fiend
watched by famished wraiths
of your self

your whole life
making money
could not pay off
death

clinging wanting
nothing on my mind
that's why I can say
it's all mine

you want someone you loved
now
only because
you never knew her

you can't forget
not to remember
someone you never forgot
who?

looking back
you see it one brief evening
realize   see
everything's a lie

bitter? does this
incredible world of grief hurt?
why wound yourself
brooding on dreams?

all this
is unreal
instead of clutching your head
go and sing

no hands   no eyes
nothing exists
touch see
that's it

your mind
yours
torments you
because you need it

hating hell
loving heaven
torture yourself
in this joyous world

the hating mind
itself is not bad
not not hating
what's bad

good   bad
crumple into a ball
of trash
for the gutter

ideas about
what you *should* do
never existed
I I I

finished
with Buddhism
nothing's
new

enlightenment   really?
"mind"
keep wrestling with yourself
idiot

these days enlightenment
means nothing to me
so I wake up
feeling fine

tired of praying
for salvation   look
those poor beautiful flowers
withering

saunter
along the river
breathe
in   out

die   live
day and night   here
listen   the world's
your hand

Buddhas
are pitiful
all dressed up   dazzled
by brocade robes

enemies
come from your mind
right wrong right wrong
never were

call it this   that
it doesn't exist
except this page
except these wandering phrases

praised   abused
like a block of wood straight through
my head's the universe
can't hide my ugliness my clumsiness

so I just go along
with what is
without anger
without happiness

nothing to see   nothing to know
before after now
call and you'll hear
its heartbreaking silence

from *Denver Quarterly*

Jealousy

◊ ◊ ◊

Attention was commanded through a simple, unadorned,
    unexplained, often decentered presence,
up to now, a margin of empty space like water, its surface
    contracting, then melting
along buried pipelines, where gulls gather in euphoric buoyancy.
    Now,
the growth of size is vital, the significance of contraction by a moat,
    a flowerbed, or
a fenced path around the reservoir, its ability to induce the mind's
    growing experience of the breadth
and depth of physical association, which turns out to be both vital
    and insufficient, because
nature never provides a border for us, of infinite elements irregularly
    but flexibly integrated,
like the rhythm between fatigue and relief of accommodation, or
    like a large apartment. Now,
the construction is not the structure of your making love to me.
    The size of your body on mine
does not equal your weight or buoyancy, like fireworks on a tele-
    vision screen, or the way
an absent double expresses inaccuracy between what exists and does
    not exist in the room,
of particular shape, volume, etc., minute areas and inferred lines we
    are talking about.
You have made a vow to a woman not to sleep with me. For me,
    it seemed enough

that love was a spiritual exercise in physical form and what was
    seen is what it was,
looking down from the twelfth floor, our arms resting on pillows
    on the windowsill. It is midnight.
Fireworks reflected in the reservoir burst simultaneously on the
    south and the north shores,
so we keep turning our heads quickly for both of the starry spheres,
instead of a tangible, and an intangible event that does not reflect.
    Certain
definite brightness contains spaciousness. A starry night, like a fully
    reflecting surface,
claims no particular status in space, or being of its own.

from *Empathy*

Crucifixion

◇ ◇ ◇

You understand the colors on the hillside have faded,
     we have the gray and brown and lavender of late autumn,
the apple and pear trees have lost their leaves, the mist
     of November is often with us, especially in the afternoon
and toward evening, as it was today when I sat gazing
     up into the orchard for a long time the way I do now,
thinking of how I died last winter and was revived.
     And I tell you I saw there a cross with a man nailed
to it, silvery in the mist, and I said to him: "Are you
     the Christ?" And he must have heard me, for in his
agony, twisted as he was, he nodded his head affirmatively,
     up and down, once and twice. And a little way off
I saw another cross with another man nailed to it,
     twisting and nodding, and then another and another,
ranks and divisions of crosses straggling like exhausted
     legions upward among the misty trees, each cross
with a silvery, writhing, twisting, nodding, naked
     figure nailed to it, and some of them were women.
The hill was filled with crucifixion. Should I not be
     telling you this? Is it excessive? But I know something
about death now, I know how silent it is, silent, even
     when the pain is shrieking and screaming. And tonight
is very silent and very dark. When I looked I saw
     nothing out there, only my own reflected head nodding

a little in the window glass. It was as if the Christ
    had nodded to me, all those writhing silvery images
on the hillside, and after a while I nodded back to him.

from *American Poetry Review*

The Life of Towns

◇ ◇ ◇

Towns are the illusion that things hang together somehow, my pear, your winter.

I am a scholar of towns, let God commend that. To explain what I do is simple enough. A scholar is someone who takes a position. From which position, certain lines become visible. You will at first think I am painting the lines myself; it's not so. I merely know where to stand to see the lines that are there. And the mysterious thing, it seems a very mysterious thing, is how these lines do paint themselves. Before there was any up or down, any bright or dark, any edges or angles or virtue—who was there to ask the questions? Well, let's not get carried away with exegesis. A scholar is someone who knows how to limit oneself to the matter at hand.

Matter which has painted itself within lines constitutes a town. Viewed in this way the world is, as we say, an open book. But what about variant readings? For example, consider the town defined for us by Lao Tzu in the twenty-third chapter of the Tao Te Ching:

A man of the way conforms to the way; a man of virtue
conforms to virtue; a man of loss conforms to loss.
He who conforms to the way is gladly accepted by the way;
he who conforms to virtue is gladly accepted by virtue;
he who conforms to loss is gladly accepted by loss.

This sounds like a town of some importance, where a person could reach beyond himself, or meet himself, as he chose. But another scholar (Kao) takes a different position on the Town of Lao Tzu. "The word translated 'loss' throughout this section does not make much sense," admonishes Kao. "It is possible that it is a graphic error for 'heaven.' " Now, in order for you or I to quit living here and go there—either to the Town of Lao Tzu or to the Town of Kao—we have to get certain details clear, like Kao's tone. Is he impatient or deeply sad or merely droll? The position you take on this may pull you separate from me. Hence, towns. And then, scholars.

I am not being trivial. Your separateness could kill you unless I take it from you as a sickness. What if you get stranded in the town where pears and winter are variants for one another? Can you eat winter? No. Can you live six months inside a frozen pear? No. But there is a place, I know the place, where you will stand and see pear and winter side by side as walls stand by silence. Can you punctuate yourself as silence? You will see the edges cut away from you, back into a world of another kind—back into real emptiness, some would say. Well, we are objects in a wind that stopped, is my view. There are regular towns and irregular towns, there are wounded towns and sober towns and fiercely remembered towns, there are useless but passionate towns that battle on, there are towns where the snow slides from the roofs of the houses with such force that victims are killed, but there are no empty towns (just empty scholars) and there is no regret.

APOSTLE TOWN

After your death.
It was windy every day.
Every day.
Opposed us like a wall.
We went.
Shouting sideways at one another.
Along the road.
It was useless.
The spaces between us.
Got hard.
They are empty spaces.
And yet they are solid.
And black and grievous.
As gaps between the teeth.
Of an old woman.
You knew years ago.
When she was.
Beautiful the nerves pouring around in her like palace fire.

Town of Spring Once Again

"Spring is always like what it used to be."
Said an old Chinese man.
Rain hissed down the windows.
Longings from a great distance.
Reached us.

Lear Town

Clamor the bells falling bells.
Precede silence of bells.
As madness precedes.
Winter as childhood.
Precedes father.
Into the kill-hole.

Desert Town

When the sage came back in.
From the desert.
He propped the disciples up again like sparrows.
On a clothesline.
Some had fallen into despair this puzzled him.
In the desert.
Where he baked his heart.
Were no shadows no up and down to remind him.
How they depended on him a boy died.
In his arms.
It is very expensive he thought.
To come back.
He began to conform.
To the cutting away ways.
Of this world a fire was roaring up.
Inside him his bones by now liquid and he saw.

Ahead of him.
Waiting nothing else.
Waiting itself.

HÖLDERLIN TOWN

You are mad to mourn alone.
With the wells gone dry.
Starlight lying at the bottom.
Like a piece of sound.
You are stranded.
Props hurtle past you.
One last thing you may believe.
Before the lights go out is.
That the mourning is at fault.
Then the sin of wishing to die.
Collapses behind you like a lung.
Night.
The night itself.

A TOWN I HAVE HEARD OF

"In the middle of nowhere."
Where.
Would that be?
Nice and quiet.
A rabbit.
Hopping across.
Nothing.
On the stove.

TOWN OF THE DEATH OF SIN

What is sin?
You asked.
The moon screamed past us.

All at once I saw you.
Just drop sin and go.
Flashing after the moon.
Black as a wind over the forests.

LOVE TOWN

She ran in.
Wet corn.
Yellow braid.
Down her back.

TOWN OF THE SOUND OF A TWIG BREAKING

Their faces I thought were knives.
The way they pointed them at me.
And waited.
A hunter is someone who listens.
So hard to his prey it pulls the weapon.
Out of his hand and impales.
Itself.

TOWN OF THE MAN IN THE MIND AT NIGHT

Twenty-five.
To four blackness no.
Waking thing no voice no wind huge.
Wads of silence stuff.
The air outside the room blackness.
Outside the streets blackness outside.
The world blackness outside blackness I wonder.
As hard as it can.
Press from deep.
In here to far.
Out there farther.

Farthest pressing out.
Where black.
Winds drop from star.
To star where the deep.
Tinkle of the moon grazes.
It knocks.
It.
Off.
The blade.
Of night like a.
Paring if a man.
Falls off the world in the dark.
Because he doesn't.
Know it is there does that mean it.
Is?

TOWN ON THE WAY THROUGH GOD'S WOODS

Tell me.
Have you ever seen woods so.
Deep so.
Every tree a word does your heart stop?
Once I saw a cloud over Bolivia so deep.
Mountains were cowering do you ever?
Look in so quick you see the secret.
Word inside the word?
As in an abandoned railway car.
One winter afternoon I saw.
The word for "God's woods."

PUSHKIN TOWN

When I live I live in the ancient future.
Deep rivers run to it angel pavements are in use.
It has rules.
And love.

And the first rule is.
The love of chance.
Some words of yours are very probably ore there.
Or will be by the time our eyes are ember.

Town of Finding Out About the Love of God

I had made a mistake.
Before this day.
Now my suitcase is ready.
Two hardboiled eggs.
For the journey are stored.
In the places where.
My eyes were.
How could it be otherwise?
Like a current.
Carrying a twig.
The sobbing made me.
Audible to you.

Death Town

This day.
Whenever I pause.
The noise of the town.

Luck own

Digging a hole.
To bury his child alive.
So that he could buy food for his aged mother.
One day.
A man struck gold.

MEMORY TOWN

In each one of you I paint.
I find.
A buried site of radioactive material.
You think 8 miles down is enough?
15 miles?
140 miles?

SEPTEMBER TOWN

One fear is that.
The sound of the cicadas.
Out in the blackness zone is going to crush my head.
Flat as a piece of paper some night.
Then I'll be expected.
To go ahead with normal tasks anyway just because.
Your head is crushed flat.
As a piece of paper doesn't mean.
You can get out of going to work.
Mending the screen door hiding.
Your brother from the police.

ENTGEGENWÄRTIGUNG TOWN

I heard you coming after me.
Like a lion through the underbrush.
And I was afraid.
I heard you.
Crashing down over flagpoles.
And I covered my ears.
I felt the walls of the buildings.
Sway once all along the street.
And I crouched low on my heels.
In the middle of the room.

Staring hard.
Then the stitches came open.
You went past.

WOLF TOWN

Let tigers.
Kill them let bears.
Kill them let tapeworms and roundworms and heartworms.
Kill them let them.
Kill each other let porcupine quills.
Kill them let salmon poisoning.
Kill them let them cut their tongue on a bone and bleed.
To death let them.
Freeze let them.
Starve let them get.
Rickets let them get.
Arthritis let them have.
Epilepsy let them get.
Cataracts and go blind let them.
Run themselves to death let eagles.
Snatch them when young let a windblown seed.
Bury itself in their inner ear destroying equilibrium let them have.
Very good ears let them yes.
Hear a cloud pass.
Overhead.

EMILY TOWN

"Riches in a little room."
Is a phrase that haunts.
Her since the voltage of you.
Left.
Snow or a library.
Or a band of angels.
With a message is.

Not what.
It meant to.
Her.

TOWN OF THE DRAGON VEIN

If you wake up too early listen for it.
A sort of inverted whistling the sound of sound.
Being withdrawn after all where?
Does all the sound in the world.
Come from day after day?
From mountains but.
They have to give it back.
At night just.
As your nightly dreams.
Are taps.
Open reversely.
In.
To.
Time.

SYLVIA TOWN

The burners and the starvers.
Came green April.
Drank their hearts came.
Burning and starving her.
Eyes pulled up like roots.
Lay on the desk.

Town of My Farewell to You

Look what a thousand blue thousand white.
Thousand blue thousand white thousand.
Blue thousand white thousand blue thousand.
White thousand blue wind today and two arms.
Blowing down the road.

Town Just Before the Lightning Flash

"Nuances not effective in point form."
Wrote Paul Klee (1923).

Town Gone to Sleep

There was distant thunder that was its.
Voice there was blood.
Hitting the ground that was.
A Creature's life melting.
In its time there.
Was air forcing.
Out to the edges of that garden as.
Veins of a diver who.
Shoots toward the surface that was a Creature's.
Hope in it just before turning to see.
Ah there we lay.
There the desert.
Of the world immense and sad as hell.
That *was* hell that.
Was a Creature's heart.
Plunged.

Town of Bathsheba's Crossing

Inside a room in Amsterdam.
Rembrandt painted a drop of life inside.
The drop he painted Rembrandt's stranger.
Dressed as a woman rippling.
With nakedness she has.
A letter in her hand she is.
Traveling.
Out of a thought toward us.
And has not yet.
Arrived even when he.
Paints Rembrandt's stranger.
As Rembrandt he shows.
Him bewildered and tousled.
As if just in.
From journeys.
On tracks and sideroads.

Anna Town

What an anxious existence I led.
And it went on for years it was years.
Before I noticed the life of objects one day.
Anna gazed down at her.
Sword I saw the sword yield up.
To her all that had been accumulated.
Within it all that strange.
World where an apple weighs more.
Than a mountain then.
We set off.
For bitter warfare.
Is dear to us.

Town of the Wrong Questions

How.
Walls are built why.
I am in here what.
Pulleys and skin when.
The panels roll back what.
Aching what.
Do they eat—light?

Freud Town

Devil say I am an unlocated.
Window of myself devil.
Say nobody sit.
There nobody light.
The lamp devil.
Say one glimpse of it.
From outside do the trick do.
The trick devil.
Say smell this devil say.
Raw bones devil say the mind.
Is an alien guest I say.
Devil outlived devil in.

Town of the Little Mouthful

Without arrows how?
Do I know if I hit.
The target he said smiling from ear.
To cut.
Through by the bowstring.

BRIDE TOWN

Hanging on the daylight black.
As an overcoat with no man in it one cold bright.
Noon the Demander was waiting for me.

JUDAS TOWN

Not a late hour not unlit rows.
Not olive trees not locks not heart.
Not moon not dark wood.
Not morsel not I.

from *Grand Street*

Wake Up

◇ ◇ ◇

In June, in the Kyborg Castle, in the canton
of Zurich, in the late afternoon, in the room
underneath the chapel, in the dungeon,
the executioner's block hunches on the floor next
to the Iron Maiden in her iron gown. Her serene features
are engraved with a little noncommittal smile. If
you ever once slipped inside her she closed her spiked
interior on you like a demon, like one
possessed. Embrace—that word on the card next to
the phrase "no escape from."
   Over in a corner stands the rack, a dream-like
contrivance that did all it was called to do, and more,
no questions asked. And if the victim passed out
too soon from pain, as his bones were being broken
one by one, the torturers simply threw a bucket of water
on him and woke him up. Woke him again
later, if necessary. They were thorough. They knew
what they were doing.
   The bucket is gone, but there's an old cherrywood
crucifix up on the wall in a corner of the room:
Christ hanging on his cross, of course, what else?
The torturers were human after all, yes? and, who
knows?—at the last minute their victim might see
the light, some chink of understanding, even acceptance of
his fate might break, might pour into his nearly molten
heart. *Jesu Christo, my Savior.*

I stare at the block. Why not? Why not indeed?
Who hasn't ever wanted to stick his neck out without fear
of consequence? Who hasn't wanted to lay his life on the line,
then draw back at the last minute?
Who, secretly, doesn't lust after every experience?
It's late. There's nobody else in the dungeon but us,
she and me, the North Pole and the South. I drop down
to my knees on the stone floor, grasp my hands behind
my back, and lay my head on the block. Inch it forward
into the pulse-filled groove until my throat fits the shallow
depression. I close my eyes, draw a breath. A deep breath.
The air thicker somehow, as if I can almost taste it.
For a moment, calm now, I feel I could almost drift off.
    Wake up, she says, and I do, turn my head over to see
her standing above me with her arms raised. I see the axe too,
the one she pretends to hold, so heavy it's all she
can do to hold it up over her shoulder. Only kidding,
she says, and lowers her arms, and the idea-of-axe, then
grins. I'm not finished yet, I say. A minute later, when I
do it again, put my head back down on the block, in
the same polished groove, eyes closed, heart racing
a little now, there's no time for the prayer forming in my
throat. It drops unfinished from my lips as I hear her
sudden movement. Feel flesh against my flesh as the sharp
wedge of her hand comes down unswervingly to the base of
my skull and I tilt, nose over chin into the last
of sight, of whatever sheen or rapture I can grasp to take
with me, wherever I'm bound.
    You can get up now, she says, and
I do. I push myself up off my knees, and I look at her,
neither of us smiling, just shaky
and not ourselves. Then her smile and my arm going
around her hips as we walk into the next corridor
needing the light. And outside then, in the open, needing more.

from *Michigan Quarterly Review*

My Cousin Muriel

◇ ◇ ◇

From Manhattan, a glittering shambles
of enthrallments and futilities, of leapers
in leotards, scissoring vortices blurred,
this spring evening, by the *punto in aria*
of hybrid pear trees in bloom (no troublesome
fruit to follow) my own eyes are drawn to—
childless spinner of metaphor, in touch
by way of switchboard and satellite, for
the last time ever, with my cousin Muriel:

mother of four, worn down by arthritis,
her kidneys wasting, alone in a hospital
somewhere in California: in that worn voice,
the redhead's sassy timbre eroded from it,
while the unspeakable stirs like a stone,
a strange half-absence and a tone of weakness
(Wordworth's discharged soldier comes to mind)
as she inquires, fatigued past irony, "How's
your work going?" As for what was hers—

nursing-home steam-table clamor, scummed
soup fat, scrubbed tubers, bones, knives,
viscera, cooking odors lived with till
they live with you, a settlement in the
olfactory tissue—well, it's my function
to imagine scenes, try for connections

as I'm trying now: a grope for words,
the numb, all but immobilized trajectory
to where my cousin, whom I've seen just once

since she went there to live, lies dying:
part of the long-drawn larger movement
that lured the Reverend Charles Wadsworth
to San Francisco, followed in imagination
from the cupola of the shuttered homestead
in Amherst where a childless recluse,
on a spring evening a century ago, A.D.
(so to speak) 1886, would cease to breathe
the air of rural Protestant New England—

an atmosphere and a condition which,
by stages, wagon trains, tent meetings,
the Revival, infused the hinterland
my cousin Muriel and I both hailed from:
a farmhouse childhood, kerosene-lit,
tatting-and-mahogany genteel. "You
were the smart one," she'd later say.
Arrant I no doubt was; as for imagining
scenes it must be she'd forgotten

the melodramas she once improvised above
the dolls' tea table: "For the pity's sake!
How could you get us all in such a fix?
Well, I s'pose we'll just have to make
the best of it"—the whole trajectory of
being female, while I played the dullard,
presaged. She bloomed, knew how to flirt,
acquired admirers. I didn't. In what I now
recall as a last teen-age heart-to-heart,

I'm saying I don't plan on getting married.
"Not ever?" "Not ever"—then, craven, "Oh,
I'd like to be *engaged*." Which is what she

would have been, by then, to Dorwin Voss,
whom I'd been sweet on in fifth grade (last
painless crush before the crash of puberty)—
blue-eyed, black-haired, good-looking Dorwin,
who'd later walk out on her and their kids,
moving on again, part of the larger exodus

from the evangel-haunted prairie hinterland.
Some stayed; the more intemperate of us
headed East—a Village basement, uptown
lunch hours, vertiginous delusions of
autonomy, the bar crowd; waiting for
some well-heeled dullard of a male to
deign to phone, or for a stumbling-
drunk, two-timing spouse's key to turn
the small-hour dark into another fracas—

others for California: the lettuce fields,
Knott's Berry Farm, the studios; palms,
slums, sprinklers, canyon landslides,
fuchsia hedges hung with hummingbirds,
the condominium's kempt squalor: whatever
Charles Wadsworth, out there, foresaw
as consolation for anyone at all—attached,
estranged, or merely marking time—little
is left, these days, these times, to say

when the unspeakable stirs like a stone.
Pulled threads, the shared fabric of a
summer memory: the state-fair campground,
pump water, morning light through tent flaps,
the promenade among the booths: blue-ribbon
zinnias and baby beeves, the cooled marvel
of a cow, life-size, carved out of butter;
a gypsy congeries without a shadow on it
but the domed torpor of the capitol

ballooning, ill at ease, egregious
souvenir of pomp among the cornfields;
Kewpie-doll lowlife along the midway,
the bleachers after dark, where, sick
with mirth, under the wanton stars,
for the ineptitude of clowns, we soared
in arabesques of phosphorus, and saw—
O dread and wonder, O initiating taste
of ecstasy—a man shot from a cannon.

Too young then to know how much we knew
already of experience, how little of
its wider paradigm, enthralled by that
punto in aria of sheer excitement, we who
are neither leaf nor bole—O hybrid
pear tree, cloned fruitless blossomer!—
suspend, uprooted from the hinterland,
this last gray filament across a continent
where the unspeakable stirs like a stone.

from *The New Yorker*

"Boys on street corners in Santa Ana . . ."

◊ ◊ ◊

Boys on street corners in Santa Ana are selling flowers, a suggestion, different for each car. You are on your way, take something. And it is on into the night like this that people go. They call from phone booths in gas stations. They hear their shoes in the cold.

Behind the restaurants, a searchlight reaches up and over.

I have spent warmer nights closer to the coast, listening to older children laughing bravely in the dark bay. The night water must have been all they could feel until a siren whined down the peninsula and they wanted to be sure of what touched them. Plumbing. Wiring. Big-eyed rodents. The people are waking up in China.

A boy picks up his plastic bucket in one hand. Parked-car radio. Restless horse.

It can't be like night to die, with the world right here—even the moon and cut of clouds, even the gradual shower on the asphalt, on the apartment roof, when down the row windows are closed against the water and someone tells someone else, who already knows, it is raining. I am not likely to sleep or die out of this.

Chinamen drink their tea. They wear loose clothes like these sheets. Into this night they are rising.

Someone starts a car below my window and pulls out under the storm. I want to know where they are going. The man in back who sells firewood is out to check his yard—a cow, ducks, one goose standing guard at the parking-lot fence.

The boys are at home in Santa Ana; their flowers are passengers in dark cars. Someone drives them and the lights go by.

from *Who Whispered Near Me*

Thinking

◇ ◇ ◇

I've thought of myself
as objective, viz,
a thing round which
lines could be drawn—

or else placed by years, the average
some sixty, say, a relative
number of months, days,
hours and minutes.

I remember thinking of war
and peace and life
for as long as I can remember.
I think we were right.

But it changes, it thinks
it can all go on forever
but it gets older.
What it wants is rest.

I've thought of place
as how long it takes
to get there and of where
it then is.

I've thought of clouds, of water
in long horizontal bodies, or
of love and women and the children
which came after.

Amazing what mind makes
out of its little pictures,
the squiggles and dots,
not to mention the words.

from *Harvard Magazine*

Dying in Your Garden of Death to Go Back into My Garden

◊ ◊ ◊

Toppled
down backward six feet through stifled heat
onto dry grass. The sacrificial
smell of grilling beef.
Telephone cables jammed with chit-chatting starlings
        make self-consciousness the sky. I
grind my spine in to know how hard I can
push toward You

without dying. God
You are this old globe Earth. Press
my cold bones back down into time's passing.
Tap Your deepest river with my spine,
my hindbrain's root. Turn
my brother's bones and my huge mother away from me.
Let me feel, in this silence of noon,
Your gold flesh.

From the jogging track's edge I kicked
a pigeon's torn-free wing into thick weeds.
Once You eat me
will You keep my flesh mute or fart wind?
The Jew next to me, sobbing
to feed his stabbed lungs air, his black-haired
torso golden with sweat,
turns his walkman up louder
—You won't
let me whisper through those headphones love's
dirge: goosestep

behind me, You mad
chattering God leaving this skull,

into the urine-scented
showers!

from *The Tyrant of the Past and the Slave of the Future*

TOM DISCH

The Crumbling Infrastructure

◇ ◇ ◇

A limb snaps, the hive is smashed, and the survivors
Buzz off to colonize another neck of the woods.
No nest is sacrosanct. Abandoned churches may serve
A while as discothèques. Steel towns may hope
To be retooled to meet the needs of foreign banks
Anxious to reinvest evaporating capital
Beyond the reach of ruin. But generally decay's
The aftermath of desuetude. Rome,
What's left of it, falls to the Hun, and all
Its noble plumbing is undone. The fountains
Of Versailles run dry, and the Bourbons are remembered
As a lower-class alternative to Scotch.
In all these matters money rules, but not as the sun,
Benign, inscrutable, and far away, but as a river would,
Collating the waters of a hundred townships,
Tolerant of dams, a source of wonder and a force
Even the Federal Reserve cannot coerce.
Basements flood, canoeists (i.e., small investors)
Drown, and nothing can be done about the mosquitoes,
But on the whole one does well to dwell in the valley.
Money, like water, yields an interest hard to deny.
Every dawn brings new quotations in the pages
Of The Times; every sunset gilds the thought of death
As though it were the mummy of a king.
Then is every man an Emerson,
Aghast at the everlasting, wild with surmise,
His daily paper dewy with the news

Of history's long, slow slouch toward
That Götterdämmerung dearest to pulp
Illustrators: Liberty's torch thrust up,
Excalibur-like, from the sands of a new Sahara
Or the waves of a new flood, her bronze flame
All that remains of Babylon. A pretty sight—
But meanwhile Liberty's toes are dry, bridges
And tunnels still traversible, and someone had better
Be paid to patch these goddamn potholes, that's all
I'm trying to say, because if they're not,
Someone's going to break an axle, and it could be one of us.

from *Southwest Review*

Of Politics, & Art

◊   ◊   ◊

Here, on the farthest point of the peninsula
The winter storm
Off the Atlantic shook the schoolhouse.
Mrs. Whitimore, dying
Of tuberculosis, said it would be after dark
Before the snowplow and bus would reach us.

She read to us from Melville.

How in an almost calamitous moment
Of sea hunting
Some men in an open boat suddenly found themselves
At the still and protected center
Of a great herd of whales
Where all the females floated on their sides
While their young nursed there. The cold frightened whalers
Just stared into what they allowed
Was the ecstatic lapidary pond of a nursing cow's
One visible eyeball.
And they were at peace with themselves.

Today I listened to a woman say
That Melville *might*
Be taught in the next decade. Another woman asked, "And why
    not?"
The first responded, "Because there are
No women in his one novel."

And Mrs. Whitimore was now reading from the Psalms.
Coughing into her handkerchief. Snow above the windows.
There was a blue light on her face, breasts and arms.
Sometimes a whole civilization can be dying
Peacefully in one young woman, in a small heated room
With thirty children
Rapt, confident and listening to the pure
God rendering voice of a storm.

from *American Poetry Review*

The Chessboard Is on Fire

◊ ◊ ◊

1

The ant stood up on two legs looks like a chesspiece maybe a bishop.

These wooden rings of different radii, stacked concentrically—make a chesspiece, which one not clear, because it's on fire, unidentifiable, unmistakable. But you don't know what we mean, we're all gangsters without a gang, fantoccini.

The stained and clear glass windows alternate. A demographic priest, full of impatient proverbs, speaks under a baldachin of twisted trees—of life—is it?

2

". . . if those shmigglaroonies that live their shithead lives in bilkoland had only once said to me, look here, shmiggle . . . then I'd have what to go on, to begin the negotiations . . ." "Shokh mat!'"

"That pligl calls everybody he knows a shmiggle." That's Italian. "Shah mat!"

("Lift up your Hefty bag and look in it midsummer when the larvae swarm and tell me if in that douchebag you don't see the provost's and the censor's scared imaginations: crowded dreams numerousness without numinousness imaginary gluts of people overpopulation smirks on shifting faces street, tunnel, wall, orange fire escape, street, crossings, tracks, another tunnel, swarming over the leftover rightover cartons and the rest to get out")

3

In a sandbank in the parish of Uig near peat moss and shipwreck
they found chesspieces, figurines, robust, humorous. The bishops
hold crozier hooks to their cheeks; some bless; some read books;
the knights grim, compact; the queens palm their faces, pin-eyed,
aghast; the kings lean forward over their swords. Scored shapes,
cornery ovals with flat bases, serve as pawns. Our pieces are more
abstract.

Rings above rings! Closed horseshoes, thrown simply, by a kilned
ghost, across the yard, the ceramist.

4

This hominid ant on two legs looks like a chesspiece: he holds a
bishopric or a rookery.

He's got a diagonal strategy—pawns massacred—massacres
pawned. All activities, no actions, half ground, Brueghel's picture,
the census at Bethlehem, activities, local accountability; and slightly
past that to a freer infinite, the other census, with no need for the
one infinite birth to offset particular births: so in the sheen of bad
demography, a poetic sheen that offsets particular shinings, the
poetries become self-appointed local juntas, amphitheaters of north-
ern dream violence, drama exiled south to machiavellian theaters.

Hey, lettuce head, you're the only narrator left. Think your way
from the migrant workers' hands to the neoconservatives' tables,
dialogue's got all the vowels starting with i, pretty green, but hey
see here they in this mercurial estuary the fish dying the they in an
alchemy of quicksilver freedoms.

5

University warden or lieutenant or whatever plant who grows in
linoleum and reads verse; complacent easy demographer "popu-
lation explosion" p's of rigged terror baby "booms"; collectivity-
designer; exponential resistance polyrhythms logistics; percussion
apocussion; eyes closed he listens to the high English holocaust

poem, savoring the September cadences (what polysemy!) nugae marketed, streaks of quotational blood. Just like that, yes just. Translation-worship and crematoria. Frieda used to say over and over: "I did not do my work." An autistic child. A diagnosis of agnosia.

"Yiddish—well. We believe in communication."

6

An ant stands up on two legs—looks around defiantly like a chess-piece.

The new moon's dark bundling says: you didn't do your job your job is to migrate.

The most important migration's perhaps from perhaps to maybe and if you ask us whether we've made it the answer's maybe.

Exempt and stet! Right in the halfmoon's face: you have no right to question us you have aphasia.

The father feared unemployment; his courage was broken. A cold Memorial day. Winter dovetails with summer.

Blacklists: long Washington wall. A fear of migration. To read Yiddish well!

7

The sun slid forced to behind the checkered clouds on the reflective umbrella over the chessmaster's head (he made his living in a dirty yellow straw hat playing in public seldom interrogated by the sergeants). He played there in University Square under a striped umbrella in the checkering rain. It was still raining. He was still winning. Someone was reading a poem by Auden there, every long line of it like the technical name of a newly instituted disease, but though the square was vibrant in the chickenshit rain that caulked the bricks with light and the hominid ants upstanding like chesspieces slid quietly toward a decent autism in old auditoriums in still worse places there was unlikely and banal torture, activity furious at not being action. Omnia migrant, one ant said. Apocussion.

8

But prose is Moses.—"We'd made a mistake and had been making it for millennia, not nihilism it was messianism and had been treeing us for god doesn't know how long and the truth is if it weren't for Moses' migratory nonmessianic ideas he had nothing to do with a messiah or for that matter if it weren't for his brother's nonmessianic staff stiff negotiatory rhetoric and empty apostrophes and empty dialogues there'd be no movement away from the slave civilization. Neither the symbols nor the negotiations saved us. Rescued not saved. He died there: migratory nonmessiah. To remain slaves we invented the idea of a messiah. The mistake: there are no translations; no messiahs, symbols of negotiation; only the empty negotiations themselves. So then we were looking out the windows of the rainrunneled shmigglaroonie cars ourselves and saw the migrant children in the fields lifting heavily as if they were trying to hoist up their parents' toys."

Now we know what you mean (of coerce, of coerce).

9

Judah and dialogue!

(Cupid's darts and the black map arrows of migration. "Let the trapped wizards who yawn in their music boxes stay there if they want to in the pawn shops." "All the board!" the three-year-old shouts joyously over his electric trains. "All the board!")

The chessboard is on fire. The flat, even squares of handcrafted wood burn evenly. No children in no fields. Rails. In the game, the king is never actually taken off, but if the board burns, the king also burns. The bishop becomes himself for the first time. The train: the terrain. You grasped it from the start (they told me about it when I was too young) so don't pretend now that this is some obscure language when all of them are private, exclusionary genocidal dialects. You are a wonderful translator. You catch the defensive truth of the original. In the well of Yiddish. Now you buried yourselves in translations instead of dialogue because it was safer to audit elsewhere than to listen to your own people, though dialogue is the wrong term for something else.

Over the mercurial estuary a kind of nonmessianic sunlight. It's not a story. The story of the stories isn't a store.

from *Boulevard*

To the Republic

◊ ◊ ◊

Past
fences the first sheepmen cast across the land, processions
of cringing pitch or cedar posts pulling into the vanishing
point like fretboards carrying barbed melodies, windharp
narratives, songs of *place,* I'm thinking of the long cowboy
ballads Ray taught me the beginnings of and would have taught
me the ends if he could have remembered them.

But remembering
was years ago when Ray swamped for ranches at a dollar a day
and found, and played guitar in a Saturday night band, and now
he is dead and I'm remembering near the end when he just needed
a drink before he could tie his shoes.

We'd stay up all night
playing the beginnings of songs like *Falling Leaf,* about a
girl who died of grief, and *Zebra Dun,* about a horse that
pawed the light out of the moon.

Sometimes Ray would break
through and recall a few more verses before he'd drop a line
or scramble a rhyme or just go blank, and his workfat hands
would drop the chords and fall away in disbelief.

Between
songs he'd pull on the rum or unleash coughing fits that
sounded like nails in a paper bag.

Done, he'd straighten and
say, *My cough's not just right, I need another cigarette,* and
light the Parliament he bit at an upward angle like Roosevelt
and play the start of another song.

Then, played out and
drunk enough to go home, he'd pick up his hat and case and
make it, usually on the second try, through the front gate
and gently list out into the early morning dark, beginning
again some song without end, yodelling his vote under spangles.

from *New Letters*

This Land

◇ ◇ ◇

1

Once upon a time (*my life had stood a loaded gun*) there was or there was not a woman (*each night I am nailed into place/and I forget who I am*) who lived in a sea of tears (*Sidra Fonseca Tonkin*). One day, for no reason she knew (*ozone layer precondition for multicellular life*), it became necessary to breathe air (*a hideous and desolate wilderness full of wild beasts and wild men*). When she raised her head above the water (*twenty Negro slaves sold to settlers*) the first absence she noticed was that of the heartbeat (*deer and bison roaming in millions passenger pigeons darkening the sky*) she had heard ever since she could (*in order not to be ashamed of my people*) remember (*Aztec Inca Pequot Wampanoag*). Her gills burned and she was lonelier (*the Americans are dropping gasoline they're going to set fire to us*) than she'd imagined possible. At dusk (*whether that nation or any nation so conceived*) she found herself on a beach, half (*the kind of girl they found dead in a hall bedroom*) in the water and half on land. A stranger (*not for us to greet each other or bid farewell we live on archipelagos*) passed, which made the woman afraid (*we thought because we had power we had wisdom*), since she didn't know a world existed (*the political entropy we face*) beyond the sea of tears she had left (*dear Father do with me what you will I am your child*). "Where do you come from?" (*in the night I took a lantern and went to see*) the stranger asked (*help me in my need and forgive the harm I do you*). She had no idea what to answer.

2

Days passed and fibers of strength (*life the sun growing hotter cries sounding*) roped her arms and legs and she traveled (*when in the course of human events it becomes*) the new country, taking a census of children (*to answer with thy uncovered body this*). At first, no matter how she tried (*then there is tear gas and we run*), she could see no children at all (*touching my face/with blind fingers of rain*); then slowly their sounds and the shapes of their faces (*I am nobody I have nothing to do with explosions*) entered her, and she counted them (*in the evening sudden thunderclaps of fear*) without much interest, noting (*our manifest destiny to overspread*) their appearance, their customs, their languages (*the* Desire *sailed from Marblehead holds partitioned into racks*). Soon this dispassionate observation (*one execution a month for the 230 remaining*) turned to resentment, then to hatred (*shelled suspected guerrilla strongholds*) of everything about them: their filthy hands (*thus were Lot's daughters with child by their father*), high voices, tears, their ridiculous size (*to pound to crush to liquidate*). Suddenly the world teemed with children (*I am born both innocent and accountable*), devouring twice their fair share of resources (*sincerely graciously trembling*), offering nothing in return (*the way you love the first person who touches you*). She abandoned the census and took a high room (*jab your spades deeper you there you others play*) where she believed they couldn't find her (*subduing a continent to the uses of civilization*). But when she closed her eyes she saw (*take my heart of stone and give me flesh*) the handwritten accounts of their lives.

3

"There was no premeditation," she insisted (*to be held by them and their children's children forever*) at the trial. "I left the tower (*in the evening there is feeling*) for apples and for company. Who (*to cut down the tree of life and make coffins*) has seen my room? Who knows my cold bed? (*I think now the worst affliction/is not to know who you are or have been*) I waited until the children were called (*detained twenty in crackdown on opponents*) for supper. The food stalls were closing. I chose (*one way to save American lives was to destroy foliage along the rivers*) three apples, and touched the grocer's hand (*if you are forsaken by all the world yet will I not forsake you*) as I offered the coins. Her eyes slid away (*who killed the pork chops? what price bananas?*). Soon I was the only woman in the street (*fair meadows goodly tall trees with such fresh waters*); the others shadowed the lit apartments (*how longing could store itself in one's bones and one day without warning*), hammering meat tender, taking soup steam (*all fruits and vegetables must be carefully washed*) in their faces. Following the sound (*wounded carried on waterproof sheets*), I found the river, where men waited (*dulce et decorum est*) for other women, the kind to roll (*to the free skies unpent glad and strong*) in the mud by the willows. As I approached (*for one people to dissolve the political bands which have bound*), several circled, young, with hard arms (*you will dance the fire dance in iron shoes*), and I felt that something completely new (*and to assume among the powers of the earth*) was about to happen. Already their beards (*I had seen birth and death/but had thought they were different*) rasped my neck, their tongues leaped between (*this wild swan of a world*) my lips, I expanded, my knees flew (*is my flesh of brass?*) open. But as I neared the clearing (*hush they're burning a nigger don't you want to see them burn a nigger*) the crowd of them parted. There lay (*I was driven to recognize that these reports were untrue*) a girl, dress bunched at her navel (*a love not unmixed with horror and anger*), smeared with semen and blood, six (*whatever happens between us your body/will haunt mine*) years old? Twelve? Seventeen? (*yes I said yes I will yes*) The men disappeared. Under closed lids (*topsoil scraped and burned*) her eyes moved. I remembered her (*Cambrian Ordovician Carboniferous*) from the census, her shrieks and the clack of her shoes (*how hard is a bullet how fragile a word*). Blood surged in my arms. Was anything ever (*I am become Death destroyer of worlds*) so simple? I opened her narrow chest (*oh Jesus Christ get me out of here dear Jesus please get me out Christ please*) with my fingers, which had become steel-strong (*let the day perish wherein I was born*), and took the heart. Here (*by any means necessary including military force*) is the evidence. Since then I have felt nothing."

At the interrogation she explained (*where does the past exist if at all*) she could not give her name, not from malice (*bloodbath inevitable bloodbath inevitable*) or principle, but because she could not (*seven million tons of American bombs*) remember. She had lost (*in Alabama a bus set afire*) all knowledge of her origins (*whose hand at the foundry whose plow in the rain*) and none of the questioner's ingenious (*pity is what one does not deny those whom one refuses to help*) persuasions could restore it, or summon (*the torment and necessity of love*) any flicker of feeling from her skin (*whatsoever a man soweth that shall he also reap*). "The child is not important," he said (*against insubordination alone we are severe*). "It is you to whom we must teach the lesson." (*that water these words what can they do what can they do*) When he entered the room where she was kept (*what passing-bells for those who die as cattle*) on the sixth day of her captivity (*a pace that opens only to tears*), she was rubbing herself with brick dust and dirt (*as they moved westward they began to die*) because the smell of her own body (*the boy looked at him and said freedom freedom*) had become unbearable to her (*upland fields the paddy the seedbeds of my village*). He took his customary position (*Shatila Sharpeville Jackson My Lai*) and she hers, stretched on the anvil floor (*an invented past can never be used*) and again he demanded her name, and persuaded (*rise like lions after slumber/in unvanquishable number*), and again she neither answered nor moved (*purple trickling along my thighs Mama's lemonade yellow runs sweet*). "Nothing?" he shouted. "Nothing? Feel (*inhabited by two .50 caliber machine guns and one man*) this," and he chopped off each of her hands (*sugar cotton indigo coffee rubber tin petroleum teak*). After that the lesson was apparently over (*and the living nations wait/each sequestered in its hate*), as the interrogator did not (*one who could go as a stranger in the village*) return, and the door was left ajar (*the long migrations meet across you and it is nothing to you you have forgotten us*). She waited for death, which did not come. Instead (*a yesterday I find almost impossible to lift*) a child appeared, running as if hunted (*corn bread tobacco smoke clay pipes copper bowls*), face hidden, holding a paper scroll (*with fifty men we could subjugate them and make them do what we want*), which was spread before her. "Listen," she was told (*chasten thy son let not thy soul spare for his crying).* "This is the map you will need. At (*in some cases they began to laugh hysterically*) the marked place is a canyon that was once (*a thoroughfare for freedom beat*) a sea. You must find it. Your hands are there." (*to me every hour of the light and dark*) The child touched her shoulder and jolts (*the shower fell sudden profuse*) of pain raced down her arms. "Do you (*please pale hot please cover rose*) understand?" the child urged. Never (*and the soul will it change? you must change it*) another question, she thought. Never (*I am bound for the land of Canaan*). Never. Never. Never. Never.

5

When neither death nor sleep would come (*to achieve our country and change the history of the world*) she set out on the seventh day (*soldiers marching afterward the road bare and white*), without much hope, and could not help (*no longer human beings in the accepted sense*) but think of the man who had questioned her (*the human voice in its calmness/in its shrillness/in its monumental invention of pitches*): the planes of his shaven cheeks, the gleam (*whom shall I seek with whom share/the heavy-hearted joy of my survival*) of sweat that filmed his forehead as he worked (*the M16 tumbles the bullet giving shorter range but a gaping wound*), how much he had asked of her (*to Thee alone every knee must bend*), how little was asked of her now. Only (*and the May month flaps its glad green leaves*) the map, riding between her belt and her side (*the first thing the dying woman feels upon return to consciousness is pain*), still demanded, with its unwieldiness and (*the specialists in our agony*) its crude, bold lines, angled toward a destination (*gas differentiated into stars galaxies planets*) that seemed inexplicably familiar (*blunt not thy heart enrage it*). Before the return of other feelings (*cobalt uranium manganese*) came hunger, and she craned her neck (*what can be expected from a commonwealth that this land affords not*) to eat fruit from tree branches, which sometimes with the wind (*to love this time for once/with all my intelligence*) moved closer to her mouth. Soon the voices (*to burn or tear or hack your way into the secret body of the other*) of everything alive became audible; when she stopped (*the bullet from his head/to make a Benin bronze*) under a pine to rest and pinned the scrolled (*the old is dying the new cannot be born*) map under her knees, she could hear (*a new nation conceived in liberty and dedicated*) the sounds of the new-fallen needles, the sap (*the point is that you are animate chattel*) rolling down the bark, the languages (*the trees of the Lord also are full even the cedars of Lebanon*) of the squirrels and the earthworms and the mosses (*people who did not believe that a child must first be conceived in a dream*). Everywhere she stepped a cry rose (*they dug and dug and thus their day/passed on and their night and they did not*). As she walked, markings stippled her arms (*at a mangle above the washroom hot steam pouring up*) and legs, letters of an alphabet (*a brass locket with a picture/of a strangled woman*) she could not read, and her eyes (*who simultaneously kept subjugated the Black sixth of their population*) blurted images: a high room (*an officer wearing a knitted skullcap who aimed his rifle at heads and hearts*) overlooking a market, children juggling apples (*rope fire fear humiliation*), a river bank with willows. As the map (*we became great students of avalanches*) predicted, the land began to flatten (*they bring you up to do like your daddy done*), but instead of desert she passed noisy riffles, streams (*with a reed stylus on unbaked clay tablets*) in spate, gulls with spear bills dropping (*demur you're straight-way dangerous/and handled with a chain*) words, until finally she shivered at the edge (*as long as grass grows or water runs*) of a sea, pitching under a storm (*nothing to give but a well-excavated grave*). All day the season had changed every hour (*Mohawk Narragansett Seneca Cherokee*); now snow lashed in the gale, and she staggered (*it is chilly on our way to the hook*) in its teeth. As the map flew from her side (*motherfatherdickandjanetheyarevery*), the voices from the sea, rhythmic (*40mm gas grenade causes immediate and copious tears*) under the irregular beat of the surf (*from all my white sins forgiven they feed*), became intelligible: weren't they (*gold diamonds ivory cocoa palm oil*) voices she had always known? Didn't they (*the land's sharp features seemed to be/the century's corpse outleant*) mean her well, wasn't that her name (*the cup of forgetfulness the waters of obliteration*) they thudded as they called her to join them? (*more in chaos without a history than we are without a future*) The waves were sucking and pounding her breasts (*too many people in the world to make oblivion possible*) before she started to feel the air crushed (*at exactly fifteen minutes past eight in the morning on August 6 1945*) from her lungs; suddenly she remembered (*I am guilty of being still alive*) the day they formed and unfurled in her chest (*igneous sedimentary metamorphic*), and all that had happened since. She battled (*I inherited Jackson Mississippi/for my majority it gave me Emmett Till*) back to shore and sank down, sobbing (*this is life then to which I am committed*), frozen clothes clattering in the wind (*brought countless and hitherto unknown ways of dying*). She fell asleep. When she woke (*my dungeon shook and my chains fell off*), the sea twitched against rocks, and snow (*the circumstances which accompany their birth affect the whole term of their being*) stretched as far as she could see (*sandy ground all over beset with fair pine trees*); strangers tended oil-barrel fires far (*clotbur sesame panic grass feverfew*) in the distance. Between her knees were clenched (*not even the weeds to multiply without blossom*) her hands, in fists. She unfolded one (*Sobibor Belzec Maidenek Chelmno*)—awkward, chapped, the tendons stiff (*when at first I liked the whites/I gave them fruits/I gave them fruits*)—and cleared a patch of sand and wrote (*as a woman I have a country*) the letters of her name.

from *Grand Street*

The Ice Age

◊   ◊   ◊

A million years ago the earth grew cold. Iowa was covered by twenty-five hundred feet of ice. No one knows why the glaciers formed and spread, or why they eventually retreated.

I blinked and you were gone.

As a boy, he loved the idea of the ice age. Lumbering woolly mammoths and giant sloths. Outside, a vast white edict erasing the landscape. Inside his head cave paintings of bison leapt in the firelight, their horns spiraling upward, the tips smoking.

Men on skis came to dig you out. Though they worked all night, they were too late.

Waking every day the frost reasserts itself. Its relentlessness a tedium, a closure. The earth must have looked more familiar when all was water. We don't recognize ourselves amidst this overwhelming winter: static that censors newscasts, cold that burns, incessant dripping as icicles perfect themselves. The night skies are a riot of Chinese silk: bolts of crimson and shadow-blue. The radio crackles faintly.

Medical refuse litters the beaches, spews into the water from a backed up sewer under the pier. Bacteria cavort in the seawater. The weather's gone haywire all over the globe. The more sensitive you are the earlier you'll die. Just hold your breath a little longer, dear.

Once you start this medication, you can't stop. Your life changes. You decide, based on a dearth of information, which force you want to submit to: *nature,* now less maternal than ever, or her idiot son—*modern medicine.* You make an effort to find some grand design in this blindness. If you can't see well enough anymore to edit your film, perhaps you can still do the music. You set an example.

Lemme outa here.

As a boy, before his mother found out and made him stop, he'd bury the frozen birds he found on the porch after big storms by warming the earth first with his father's blowtorch.

Being human, we can't help attempting to arrange events into patterns—the way a sick man sees faces in the stains on his bedroom ceiling. He names then. Months later, they all converse.

The men in the ice-covered radio station play cards and drink bourbon.

What defense can one mount against an avalanche?

Spotless beakers, pipettes, rows of small cages. Welcome to the lab. Here's the chamber where we run preliminary screenings. Better don these gloves. Why not use two pair, like me? The new man on the night shift nods off over his work, with the radio playing. Its tinned strands of music enter his dream disguised as a dead friend's hair. He had short, coarse hair, like a terrier, pleasantly stiff to the touch. The lab is brightly lit to ward off the backwash of night. Under the table the research assistant's feet twitch spasmodically in his sleep.

A series of blurry, black-and-white newsreels flickers on screen. Martian canals overflow their banks. A lake in Africa exhales a cloud of poison gas, killing thousands of villagers on its shores. Venice sinks. Anchorage, Alaska, is leveled by earthquakes. Pompeii is breaded and fried by its volcano. The swamp swallows another sand bar, then coughs up a tiny island. Sub-zero temperatures paralyze Acapulco. *There have been several ice ages* a female narrator intones. *The most recent lasted 90,000 years.* A timer goes off and the lab assistant jerks awake. In about the time it takes to drink a glass of water, he remembers where he is.

"This is probably the last time I will write to you . . ."

The rocks applaud. Summers turn short and cool. The world remakes itself without us now.

from *The Paris Review*

The War

◇ ◇ ◇

We were at the border and they were checking
the luggage. We had been talking about Lermontov's
novel, *A Hero of Our Time*. John liked Petorin
because he was so modern during that transition
from one history to another. I talked about Vera
and Princess Mary, the old man and the others
Petorin hurt. I said there was no reckoning,
that he was not made accountable as in Tolstoy
or Dostoevsky. Maybe morality does change,
I was thinking, but suffering does not. Then
a scorpion crawled from a satchel on the table.
He fell to the floor and scurried across the room.
The men were delighted. One crouched down and held
the scorpion with a ballpoint pen while he cut off
the poisoned stinger at the end of the tail.
The scorpion stretched out was as long as a hand.
The men gathered around, their open pocket knives
held shoulder high. The man picked up the scorpion
by the tail and put it on his friend who yelped,
jumping. The men laughed. The scorpion fell.
Another man picked it up and threw it lightly
against the wall. The scorpion fell and kept trying,
scuttling across the tiles toward the open door.
He kept his tail high, threatening, but looked tired.

There was excitement in the men, and happiness.
Somebody else picked up the scorpion and I told John
I was going. We went outside where there was nothing.

from *New Letters*

Duncan

◇ ◇ ◇

1

When in his twenties a poetry's full strength
Burst into voice as an unstopping flood,
He let the divine prompting (come at length)
Rushingly bear him any way it would
And went on writing while the Ferry turned
From San Francisco, back from Berkeley too,
And back again, and back again. He learned
You add to, you don't cancel what you do.

Between the notebook-margins his pen traveled,
His own lines carrying him in a new mode
To ports in which past purposes unraveled.
So that, as on the Ferry Line he rode,
Whatever his first plans that night had been,
The energy that rose from their confusion
Became the changing passage lived within
While the pen wrote, and looked beyond conclusion.

2

Forty years later, and both kidneys gone;
Every eight hours, home dialysis;
The habit of his restlessness stayed on
Exhausting him with his responsiveness.

After the circulations of one day
In which he taught a three-hour seminar
Then gave a reading clear across the Bay,
And while returning from it to the car

With plunging hovering tread tired and unsteady
Down Wheeler steps, he faltered and he fell
—Fell he said later, as if I stood ready,
"Into the strong arms of Thom Gunn."
                              Well well,
The image comic, as I might have known,
And generous, but it turned things round to myth:
He fell across the white steps there alone,
Though it was me indeed that he was with.

I hadn't caught him, hadn't seen in time,
And picked him up where he had softly dropped,
A pillow full of feathers. Was it a rime
He later sought, in which he might adopt
The role of H.D., broken-hipped and old,
Who, as she moved off from the reading-stand
Had stumbled on the platform but was held
And steadied by another poet's hand?

He was now a posthumous poet, I have said
(For since his illness he had not composed),
In sight of a conclusion, whose great dread
Was closure,
                his life soon to be enclosed
Like the swallow's flight above the feasting friends,
Briefly revealed where its breast caught their light,
Beneath the long roof, between open ends,
Themselves the margins of unchanging night.

from *The Threepenny Review*

Praise for Death

◇ ◇ ◇

1

Let us praise death that turns pink cheeks to ashes,
that reduces father from son and daughter, that sets tears
in the tall widow's eye. Let us praise death that gathers
us loose-limbed and weeping by the grave's edge in the flat
yard near the sea that continues. Let us praise death

2

that fastens my body to yours and renders skin
against skin sometimes intolerably sweet, as October
sweetens the flesh of a McIntosh apple. Let us praise
death that prints snapshots, fixing an afternoon forty
years ago on a sandy lane. While we stand holding

3

each other, let us praise death as a dog praises
its master, bowing, paying obeisance, rolling over;
let us praise death as a spaniel praises a pitbull.
What remained of her at the end, compared to my friend
eight months before, was the orange peel to the orange:

as if the shard of fruit—once pungent and moist, now smeared
with coffeegrounds—pulsed, opened an eye, and screamed
without stopping. As we enter the passage of agony,
imagining darkness prepared underground, we recollect
Jesus who drank from the cup: "Why have you forsaken me?"

5

Praising death we sing parts with Between-the-Rivers,
with the King of Uruk, dole's aboriginal singer.
The Victorian with his imperial figleaf praises death
like the Inca, or like the first emperor of Qin
who models a deathless army in terra cotta. Let us

praise rictus and the involuntary release of excrement
as the *poilu* does, and Attila, and the Vestal Virgin.
We remember the terrified face behind the plexiglass mask
as Hadrian remembers Antinous. Are you rich, young,
lucky, and handsome? Are you old and unknown?

7

Are you Mesopotamian, suburbanite, Cossack, Parisian?
We praise death so much, we endow our children with it.
At seventy-eight, Henry Adams spent the summer of 1916
discussing with Brooks "the total failure of the universe,
most especially *our* country." From London he heard

8

that Harry James was dead, who "belonged to my wife's set,"
he wrote Elizabeth Cameron, "and you know how I cling
to my wife's set." Thirty years before, he discovered Clover,
still warm, her lips damp with potassium cyanide.
"All day today," he wrote, "I have been living in the '70s."

9

By the river abandoned factories tilt like gravestones,
Mills collapse behind broken windows over soil broken
to build them, where millhands wore their lives out
standing in fractured noisy stench among endless belts
and hoses steaming waste to the fish-killing river.

10

Commerce dies, and commerce raises itself elsewhere.
If we read the Boston *Globe* on a Monday, we find fixed
to the business section the part-index: *Deaths, Comics.*
The old father's dignity, as he daily and hourly rehearses
the lines of his pain, stiffens him into a tableau vivant.

11

All day he studies the script of no-desire, scrupulous
never to want what he cannot have. He controls speech,
he controls desire, and a young man's intense blue eyes
look from his face as he asks his grandniece to purchase,
at the medical supply store, rubber pants and disposable pads.

12

Let us praise death that raises itself to such power
that nothing but death exists: not breakfast nor the Long
Island Expressway, not cigarettes nor beaches at Maui,
not the Tigers nor sunrise except under the aspect
of death. Let us praise death that recedes: One day

13

we realize, an hour after waking, that for a whole hour
we have forgotten the dead, so recently gone underground,
whom we swore we would mourn from the moment we opened
our eyes. All night in sleep I watch as the sinewy, angry
body careers and hurtles in harmless air, hovering

14

like a hang glider over the western slope of Kearsarge,
fired from the Porsche that explodes, rips open, settles,
and burns while the body still twists in the air, arms
akimbo, Exxon cap departing frail skull, ponytail out
straight, until it ends against granite. Let us praise

15

death that bursts skull, lungs, spleen, liver, and heart.
Let us praise death for the piano player who quit high school
in 1921 and played *le jazz hot* through France and Italy;
who recorded with *Lud Gluskin et son Jazz* four hundred
sides of a barrelhouse left hand; who jammed with Bix

16

at Walled Lake in 1930; who tinkled foxtrots for Goldkette
and Weems, suitcase depression nights of Wilkes-Barre
and Akron; who settled down to play clubs, give lessons,
run the musician's Local, and when he died left
a thousand books behind, with the markers still in them.

17

Let us praise the death of dirt. The builder tells us
that the most effective way to preserve topsoil
is to pave it over. Petersen's farm in Hamden raised
corn, beans, and tomatoes for sale at New Haven's markets.
For a hundred years they ripened in Adams Avenue's

18

countryside among the slow cattle of dairy farms.
Now slopes extrude hairy antennae; earth conceals itself
under parking lots and the slimy, collapsing sheds
of STOP & SHOP, BROOKS, BOB'S, CALDOR, and CRAZY EDDIES.
The empire rots turning brown. Junkyards of commerce

19

slide into tar over dirt impervious to erosion, sun, wind,
and the breaking tips of green-leafed, infrangible corn.
Beside his right eye and low on his neck shiny patches of skin
blaze the removed cancer. The fifty-year-old poet and I
drink seltzer together in the Grasshopper Tavern; he rants

like Thersites denouncing his Greeks. Probably it won't
kill him, but toadstool up each year: *"I want"*—he looks
longingly; desire remakes his face—*"I want so much to die."*
Let us never forget to praise the deaths of animals:
The young red tomcat—long-haired, his tail like a fox's,

with bird feathers of fur upstarting between his toes,
who emitted a brief squeak of astonishment, like the sound
squeezed from a rubber doll, when he jumped to the floor
from a high bookcase; who rattled a doorknob trying to open
a door for himself; who, if we then opened the same door,

declined our absurd, well-meaning suggestion that he use it;
who bounced and never walked; who moused assiduously
and lacking mice ripped out carpet pads for swatting;
who spend most waking hours birdwatching from the pantry
window; who sprawled upside down in our arms, splaying

long legs stiffly out, great ruffled tail dangling—
abruptly wasted and died of liver failure: We buried him
this morning by the barn, in the cat's graveyard
under blue asters, tamping dirt down over a last red ear.
Downstairs her nieces gather weeping among soft chairs

24

while neighbors bring casseroles and silence;
in the bedroom the widower opens the closet door
where her dresses hang, and finds one hanger swaying.
At Blackwater Farm beside Route 4 the vale bellies
wide from the river, four hundred acres of black dirt

25

over glacial sand, where Jack and his uncles spread
a century of cow manure. They milked their cattle
morning and night, feeding them grain, silage, and hay
while the renewable sisters drank at the river's edge,
chewed cuds, bore yearly calves, bounced and mooed

26

to praise each other's calving, and produced a frothing
blue-white Atlantic of Holstein milk. Yesterday the roads
went in, great yellow earthmachines dozing through loam
to sand, as Jack's boy Richard raises fifty Colonial Capes
with two-car garages and driveways, RIVERVIEW MEADOW FARMS

27

over smothered alluvial soil. "Death tends to occur,"
as the Professor actually said, "at the end of life."
When I heard that his daughter coming home from her job
found Clarence cold in his bed, I remembered the veiny
cheeks and laconic stories: For one moment I mourned him.

28

Then I felt my lungs inflate themselves deeply, painfully:
I imagined my own body beneath the disordered quilt.
For the first time in a year I felt myself collapse
under the desire to smoke. Like you, I want to die:
We praise death when we smoke, and when we stop smoking.

29

After the farmer fired him, the drunk farmhand returned
at nightfall and beat him to death with a tire iron
while his wife and six-year-old son stood watching.
As his father's body flopped in the wet sand, as blood
coiled out of ears, the boy—who had observed

30

hens without heads, stuck pigs, and a paralyzed mule
twitching in a stall—cried, "Die! Please die. Please."
Let us praise St. Nihil's Church of the Suburban Consensus;
at St. Nihil's we keep the coffin closed for the funeral;
when we take communion at St. Nihil's, the Euphemism melts

31

in our mouths: *pass, pass away, sleep, decease, expire.*
Quickly by shocking fire that blackens and vanishes,
turning insides out, or slowly by fires of rust and rot,
the old houses die, the barns and outbuildings die.
Let us praise death that removes nails carpenters hammered

during the battle of Shiloh; that solves the beam-shape
an adze gave an oak tree; that collapses finally
the settler's roof into his root cellar, where timber sawn
two centuries ago rots among weeds and saplings. Let us
praise death for the house erected by skill and oxen.

33

Let us praise death in old age. Wagging our tails,
bowing, whimpering, let us praise sudden crib-death
and death in battle: Dressed in blue the rifleman charges
the granite wall. Let us praise airplane crashes.
We buried thirty-year-old Stephen the photographer

34

in Michigan's November rain. His bony widow Sarah, pale
in her loose black dress, leaned forward impulsively
as the coffin, suspended from a yellow crane, swayed
over the hole. When she touched the shiny damp maple
of the box, it swung slightly away from her

35

as it continued downard. Stephen's mother Joan
knelt first to scrape wet dirt onto the coffin lid;
then his father Peter lifted handfuls and let them drop,
then his sister Sarah, then his widow Sarah. Under
scraggly graveyard trees, five young gravediggers stood

smoking together, men tattooed and unshaven, wearing
baseball caps, shifting from foot to foot, saying
nothing, trying never to watch in Michigan's November rain.
"Bitterly, bitterly I weep for my blood-brother Enkidu.
Should I *praise* master death that commanded my friend?

37

"I wander hunting in the forest weeping salt tears;
in my anger I slaughter the deer. Bitterly I cry:
'Nowhere can I lay my head down to rest or to sleep!
Despair sucks my liver out! Desolation eats bitter meat
from my thigh! What happened to my brother will happen to me.'

38

"I stood by his body eight days. I implored him to throw
death over, to rise and pull his gold breastplate on.
On the ninth day worms crawled from the skin of his neck.
Now, therefore, I climb to the sun's garden, to Utnapishtim
who alone of all men after the flood lives without dying."

from *The Gettysburg Review*

Bell & Capitol

◇ ◇ ◇

There is the sound of trumpets brilliant off the brick
of the treasury building, and later the fine, shrill resonance
of a small bell struck at noon with a silver mallet.

The jade dragonflies hover over the swamp
and the women return from the fields,
vessels of water balanced on their heads.

The echoes of the Legions ring down the dirt-packed roads
that circle the outskirts of the city, the soldiers
aloof, stiff in their armor, the horses trotting

sideways through the vegetable and fruit stands.
The sun off the breastplates of the soldiers
is brilliant, like the perfect, high-pitched

sound of the noon bell, the muezzin here, calling back
the devoted who arrive like breakers riding in
off tidal information, rising at first, filling,

then failing into the shallows, pulled back
beyond the buoys of the outer bay whose bells
gently announce the first ships at anchor.

from *Ontario Review*

Berkeley Eclogue

◇ ◇ ◇

1.

Sunlight on the streets in afternoon
and shadows on the faces in the open-air cafés.
What for? Wrong question. You knock
without knowing that you knocked. The door
opens on a century of clouds and centuries
of centuries of clouds. The bird sings
among the toyons in the spring's diligence
of rain. *And then what? Hand on your heart.*
Would you die for spring? What would you die for?
Anything?
       Anything. It may be I can't find it
and they can, the spooners of whipped cream
and espresso at the sunny tables, the women
with their children in the stores. *You want to sing?*
Tra-la. Empty and he wants to sing.
A pretty river, but there were no fish.
Smart fish. They will be feeding for a while.
He wants to sing. Yes, poverty or death.
Piety or death, you meant, you dope. You fool,
"bloody little fool." She slammed the door.
He was, of course, forlorn. And lorn and afterlorn.
It made a busy afternoon. The nights were difficult.
No doors, no drama. The moon ached aimlessly.
Dogs in the morning had their dog masks on.
It did not seem good, the moths, the apples?

The gold meander in her long brown hair
cast one vote then, sinuous as wrists. He attended
to her earnestness as well—and the child liked breakfast.
He believed in that. Every day was a present
he pretended that he brought. The sun came up.
Nothing to it. I'll do it again tomorrow,
and it did. Sundays he fetched croissants,
the frank nipples of brioche that say it's day,
eat up, the phone will ring, the mail arrive.
Someone who heard you sing the moths, the apples,
and they were—for sure they were, and good
though over there. Gold hair. A lucky guy
with a head on his shouders, and all heart.
You can skip this part. The moths, the apples,
and the morning news. Apartheid, terror,
boys in a jungle swagging guns. *Injustice
in tropical climates is appalling,
and it does do you credit to think so.*
I knew that I had my own work to do.
The ones who wear the boots decide all that.
He wants to sing one thing so true that it is true.
I cast a vote across the river, skipped another
on the pond. It skittered for a while triumphantly,
then sank. And we were naked on the riverbank.
I believed a little in her breasts, the color
of the aureoles that afternoon, and something
she said about her sister that seemed shrewd.
Afterward we watched a woman making masks,
mostly with feathers and a plaster cast of face
she glued them to. The mouths formed cries.
They were the parts that weren't there—implied
by what surrounded them. They were a cunning
emptiness. *I think you ought to start again.*
The fish were smart. They mouthed the salmon eggs,
or so you felt. The boys kept reeling in.
Casting and reeling in. You'll never catch a fish
that way, you said. One caught a fish that way.
One perched in a chair abandoned on the sand.

Drank orange soda, watched his rod twitter
in a fork of willow twig. "I'm getting a bite, Dad."
It was the river current or the wind. In every
language in the world, I bet. *Do you believe
in that?* Not especially. It means the race is old.
And full of hope? *He wants to sing.*
You bastard, she said, and slammed the door.
You've been in this part already. Say "before."
"Before." She shut the door. It couldn't have been
otherwise. How sick you were. The mouths, the apples,
the buttons on a blouse. The bone was like pearl,
and small, and very shiny. The fat child's face
was flecked with Santa Rosa plum. She cried.
Her mother hit her. Then it seemed like blood.
A flood of tears, then. You remembered
never to interfere. It humiliates them.
They beat the child again when they get home.
It's only your feeling you assuage.
You didn't interfere. Her gold wandering of hair,
she told you that another time. The father
at the county fair was wailing on the boy
with fists. There was music in the background
and a clown walked by and looked and looked away.
She told you then, gold and practical advice.
You wanted one and craved the other.
Say "mother." No. *Say it.* No. *She shut the door?*
I wish she had. I saw the shadow cast there
on the floor. *What did you think?* I asked her,
actually. She said she hurt her lip. And
took a drink? Or the shadow did. I didn't think.
I knew she was lying. A child could see that.
You were a child. *Ah, this is the part
where he parades his wound. He was a child.*
It is the law of things: the little billy goat
goes first. Happily, he's not a morsel
for the troll. *Say "Dad, I've got a bite."*
That's different. Then you say, "Reel it in."
They're feeling fear and wonder, then.

That's when you teach them they can take the world
in hand. *You do?* Sometimes I do. Carefully.
They beat the child again when they get home.
All right. Assume the children are alright.
They're singing in the kibbutzim. The sun is rising.
Let's get past this part. The kindergarten
is a garden and they face their fears in stories
your voice makes musical and then they sleep.
They hear the sirens? *Yes, they hear the sirens.*
That part can't be helped. No one beats them, though.
And there are no lies they recognize. They know
you're with them and they fall asleep. What then?
Get past this part. It is a garden. Then they're grown.
What then? Say "groan." I say what to say,
you don't. They all ok, and grown. What then?

2.

Then? Then, the truth is, then they fall in love.
Oh no. *Oh yes.* Big subject. *Big shadow.*
I saw it slant across the floor, linoleum
in fact, and very dirty. Sad and dirty.
Because it lacked intention? Well, it did lack art.
Let's leave the shadow part alone. They fall in love.
What then? I want to leave this too.
It has its songs. Too many. I know them all.
It doesn't seem appropriate somehow. It was summer.
He saw her wandering through a field of grass.
It was the sweetest fire. Later, in the fall, it rained.
You loved her then? In rain? and gold October?
I would have died for her. *Tra-la.* Oh yes,
tra-la. We took long walks. You gather sadness
from a childhood to make a gift of it.
I gave her mine. *Some gift.* Is it so bad?
Sadness is a pretty word. Shadow's
shadow. And once there was a flood. Heavy rains,
and then the tide came in. I left her house

at midnight. It was pouring. I hitched a ride,
which stalled. The car in front of us had stopped.
The water rose across the road and ran downhill.
You'd forgotten this. I remember now. My knee
was in a cast. I hopped to the car in front,
the one that stalled. The driver's tongue stuck out,
a pale fat plum. His eyes bulged. An old man
in a gray felt hat. And the red lids flickered,
so he wasn't dead. *What did you do?* Got in,
shoved him aside, and tried to start the car.
What did you feel then? Wonderful. Like cleaning fish.
Your hands are bloody and you do the job.
It reminds you of a poem now? Yes,
the one about the fall that Bashō liked.
"The maple leaf becomes a midwife's hand."
The engine skipped and sank, twice. Then it started.
And I drove. The hospital was just a mile away
but near the creek. I thought the water
would be even higher. *Interesting, of course.*
This is the part about falling in love?
I left her house. We were necking, remember,
on a soft green velvet couch. *What then?*
I took the downhill road and floored it.
A gush spewed up and blurred the windshield.
I couldn't see a thing. The car sputtered,
surged, sputtered, surged, and died. And
he was dead. *Who was he?* Some old man.
That was the winter that you fell in love?
It was. *Did you feel bad?* No, I tried.
Do you believe in that? Now? I'm not sure.
He looked like a baby when they got him out
and raindrops bounced off raindrops on his face.
It didn't cost me anything.
                                      Anything?

from *Human Wishes*

84

Crossings

◇ ◇ ◇

On St. Brigid's Day the new life could be entered
By going through her girdle of straw rope.
The proper way for men was right leg first,

Then right arm and right shoulder, head, then left
Shoulder, arm, and leg. Women drew it down
Over the body and stepped out of it.

The open they came into by these moves
Stood opener, hoops came off the world,
They could feel the February air

Still soft above their heads and imagine
The limp rope fray and flare like windborn gleanings
Or an unhindered goldfinch over plowland.

────────────

Not an avenue and not a bower.
For a quarter mile or so, where the county road
Is running straight across North Antrim bog,

Tall old fir trees line it on both sides.
Scotch firs, that is. Calligraphic shocks
Bushed and tufted in prevailing winds.

You drive into a meaning made of trees.
Or not exactly trees. It is a sense
Of running through and under without let,

Of glimpse and dapple. A life all trace and skim
The car has vanished out of. A fanned nape
Sensitive to the millionth of a flicker.

———————

Running water never disappointed.
Crossing water always furthered something.
Stepping stones were stations of the soul.

A kesh could mean the track some called a causey
Raised above the wetness of the bog,
Or the part of it that bridged old drains and streams.

It steadies me to tell these things. Also
I cannot mention keshes or the ford
Without my father's shade appearing to me

On a path toward sunset, eying spades and clothes
That turf-cutters stowed perhaps or souls cast off
Before they crossed the log that spans the burn.

———————

Be literal a moment. Recollect
Walking out on what had been emptied out
After he died, turning your back and leaving.

That morning tiles were harder, windows colder,
The raindrops on the pane more scourged, the grass
Barer to the sky, more wind-harrowed,

Or so it seemed. The house that he had planned—
"Plain, big, straight, ordinary, you know?"—
A paradigm of rigor and correction,

Rebuke to fanciness and shrine to limit,
Stood firmer than ever for its own idea,
Like a printed X-ray for the X-rayed body.

———————

To those who have seen spirits, human skin
For a long time afterward appears most coarse.
The face I see that all falls short of since

Passes down an aisle: I share the bus
From San Francisco airport into Berkeley
With one other passenger, who's dropped

At Treasure Island military base,
Halfway across Bay Bridge, Vietnam-bound,
He could have been one newly dead come back,

Unsurprisable but still disappointed,
Having to bear his farm-boy self again,
His shaving cuts, his otherworldly brow.

Shaving cuts. The pallor of bad habits.
Sunday afternoons, when summer idled
And couples walked the road along the Foyle,

We brought a shaving mirror to our window
In the top story of the boarders' dorms:
Lovers in the happy valley, cars

Eager-backed and silent, the absolute river
Between us and it all. We tilted the glass up
Into the sun and found the range and shone

A flitting light on what we could not have.
Brightness played over them in chancy sweeps
Like flashes from a god's shield or the gene pool.

And yes, my friend, we, too, walked through a valley.
Once. In darkness. With all the street lamps off.
When scaresome night made *valley* of that town.

Scene from Dante, made more memorable
By one of his head-clearing similes—
Fireflies, say, since the policemen's torches

Clustered and flicked and tempted us to trust
The unpredictable, attractive light.
We were like herded shades who had to cross

And did cross, in a panic, to the car
Parked as we'd left it, that gave when we got in
Like Charon's boat under the faring poets.

from *The New Yorker*

ANTHONY HECHT

Eclogue of the Shepherd and the Townie

◇ ◇ ◇

SHEPHERD

Not the blue-fountained Florida hotel,
Bell-capped, bellevued, straitjacketed and decked
With chromium palms and a fromage of moon,
Not goodnight chocolates, nor the soothing slide
Of huîtres and sentinel straight-up martinis,
Neither the yacht heraldic nor the stretch
Limos and pants, Swiss banks or Alpine stocks
Shall solace you, or quiet the long pain
Of cold ancestral disinheritance,
Severing your friendly commerce with the beasts,
Gone, lapsed, and canceled, rendered obsolete
As the gonfalon of Bessarabia,
The shawm, the jitney, the equestrian order,
The dark daguerreotypes of Paradise.

TOWNIE

No humble folding cot, no steaming sty
Or sheep-dipped meadow now shall dignify
Your brute and sordid commerce with the beasts,
Scotch your flea-bitten bitterness or down
The voice that keeps repeating, "Up your *Ars*

89

Poetica, your earliest diapered dream
Of the long-gone Odd Fellows amity
Of bunny and scorpion, the *entente cordiale*
Of lamb and lion, the old nursery fraud
And droll Aesopic zoo in which the chatter
Of chimp and chaffinch, manticore and mouse,
Diverts us from all thought of entrecôtes,
Prime ribs and rashers, filet mignonnettes,
Provided for the paired pythons and jackals,
Off to their catered second honeymoons
On Noah's forty-day excursion cruise."

SHEPERD

Call it, if this should please you, but a dream,
A bald, long-standing lie and mockery,
Yet it deserves better than your contempt.
Think also of that interstellar darkness,
Silence and desolation from which the Tempter,
Like a space capsule exiled into orbit,
Looks down on our green cabinet of peace,
A place classless and weaponless, without
Envy or fossil fuel or architecture.
Think of him as at dawn he views a snail
Traveling with blind caution up the spine
Of a frond asway with its little inching weight
In windless nods that deepen with assent
Till the ambler at last comes back to earth,
Leaving his route, as on the boughs of heaven,
Traced with a silver scrawl. The morning mist
Haunts all about that action till the sun
Makes of it a small glory, and the dew
Holds the whole scale of rainbow, the accord
Of stars and waters, luminously viewed
At the same time by water-walking spiders
That dimple a surface with their passages.
In the lewd Viennese catalogue of dreams
It's one of the few to speak of without shame.

TOWNIE

It is the dream of a shepherd king or child,
And is without all blemish except one:
That it supposes all virtue to stem
From pure simplicity. But many cures
Of body and of spirit are the fruit
Of cultivated thought. Kindness itself
Depends on what we call consideration.
Your fear of corruption is a fear of thought,
Therefore you would be thoughtless. Think again.
Consider the perfect hexagrams of snow,
Those broadcast emblems of divinity,
That prove in their unduplicable shapes
Insights of Thales and Pythagoras.
If you must dream, dream of the ratio
Of Nine to Six to Four Palladio used
To shape those rooms and chapels where the soul
Imagines itself blessed, and finds its peace
Even in chambers of the *Malcontenta,*
Those just proportions we hypostatize
Not as flat prairies but the City of God.

from *The Sewanee Review*

On Nothing

◇　◇　◇

The problem is the dissection problem.
Let me have at that frog. One lays open
a tiny heart and slimy little lungs
and is sickened by bullfrogs mottled in pond water,
mating forever. Is it too much or too little love
for the world that moves one to despair
in this life about the despair of nothing after life,
which this life briefly—badly—interrupts?

It is true, nothing is unfamiliar to us,
accustomed as we are to linoleum, wool snoods,
hands in pockets feeling the working hip bone.
But nothing is not despair, nor dark, nor pain;
it is none of these, and that is the point.
So if driven by fear of nothing, despair
is a simple mistake, a bit of a joke.

And what a waste of the gaping something to think
that because it is over soon, it is a groaning
effort to haul the sun each morning, to scurry
around a pyramid of footstools, improbable beings
frantic as mimes to prop up marvels that wobble
toward drains or manholes.

And too, it's unclear that eternity
has claim to meaning, or that if we had longer—
forever say—we could do better than we do

at five in a wagon, at eighty brushing the hair
from the forehead of a new youth.
Eternity seems an unlikely place to look
for more. Those twin prongs of before and after
seem merely to hold the middle ground like skewers
on summer corn so we may bring it tidily to our lips.

In fact, we don't know that there is nothing.
All that we are and all that we aren't—it's not that.
The process of oceans grinding shells to sand
and sucking it back for bottom dwellers—it's not
even that. Zero is our invention,
an idea for which there is no evidence.
The great metaphor of empty space is false,
full of red suns rising in every direction.
A vacuum is light. A leg severed is memory.
A child unborn is regret or relief.
An accident avoided is a picnic by the road
with Dairy Queen burgers in thin tissue wrappings
smelling of salt and blissful grease.

Except that we think of it, and on occasion,
groping for a nameless quarter, will feel the pull
of a thing beyond reckoning. But to think of it,
even to name it nameless means: *that* is not what we face.
Either our minds are famously unreliable
and we should get on with folding napkins and sheets
steaming from the iron, or our thoughts
are not aliens, rather emitted from nature like shad roe,
oxides, uranium and burls. If so, these
conceptual visions of nothing, at which we excel,
are pictures of home, to be admired more stringently.

from *The Hudson Review*

No Greener Pastures

◇ ◇ ◇

for Naomi

Under stress the great hawk circles,
holding greenness in its eye;
under stress the greenness travels; and under
stress the eye perceives this,
making chemicals to lift the spring;

but I have taught all morning
Hypothesis, Inductive Leap
until the mind had within it
no questions,
and no leaping,

though one kid has written, for my benefit,
"The hills have a certain
greenness about them." And another:
"Nature as a hole is beautiful. . . ."

Where is there a better place than this?
What we want is simply past our reach.
I drive back home through the beloved hills
and always the same image comes to me:
the sight of a Victorian lady
shifting under her coverlet,
the sense that beauty is too far away.

No one behind me now; I pull over,
the sleek white flanks of my Toyota glint in the
      mirror.
Half a mile from Inspiration Point, black loops:
the hawk circles the dead thing, like an English
      teacher.

An hour ago the students did the midterm,
produced the knotted writing
like saved string; I heard
the whispered thumping of a ballpoint
as it hit the page
inside the hamster cage of an Idea—

they looked up—something was missing!—I looked
      out

to the green hills, longing to be there,
and thought I saw, beneath the anorexic cross,
some crawling human speck,
the little pioneer!

Gold glints in vectors off the mission in the suburbs,
the Virgin implores in the alcove—
always the impediment here.
Always language first
and then the hills. The lover,
then the avatar. Shall we tell
the students *that?*
There's a gap between the spirit and the world
and nothing nothing
ever fills it up!

In 1962, on my mother's Remington,
I typed the novel, *No Greener Pastures.*
An earnest girl, full of ardor,
led the wagon train. Love came

and went like malaria;
there was a birth, a wedding, or a death on every
    page,

and how pleasantly disasters pressed up
through that blue typescript, single-spaced: snakebites
through muslin, the nightly circle
of disease and complaint—
but writing was like reaching
California—the absolute condition
with a beach—

I want her back, that sweet commuter.
She stayed in a shawl, chapter 16, eking out
    dialogue. . . .
The car coughs a little, loaded with essays.
I go the back way, turning out to rest
at the gritty, lovely U. My colleague
takes the brave route back to camp; after the meeting
I saw her clutch the wheel, and squint
before she drove onto the ramp, her immigrant
braids curved gracefully the way
she had to pull upward through the rather
meaningless arrows—

from *Fortress*

JOHN HOLLANDER

An Old-Fashioned Song

◇　◇　◇

("Nous n'irons plus au bois")

No more walks in the wood:
The trees have all been cut
Down, and where once they stood
Not even a wagon rut
Appears along the path
Low brush is taking over

No more walks in the wood;
This is the aftermath
Of afternoons in the clover
Fields where we once made love
Then wandered home together
Where the trees arched above,
Where we made our own weather
When branches were the sky.
Now they are gone for good,
And you, for ill, and I
Am only a passer-by.

We and the trees and the way
Back from the fields of play
Lasted as long as we could.
No more walks in the wood.

from *The New Republic*

Climbing Out of the Cage

◇ ◇ ◇

After the official exchange, when all
The sacrifices stepped out of official uniform,
When the matter was simply stated,
We sat to examine what was desperately
Trying to make the day shorter. The prize
Of this was that the night came to be considerably longer.
Not a small consolation. It would also seem
The hours had gained a limpid disposition
Amidst the chaos of this consideration.
And so, a certain surrender came to mark the sessions.

(My name is Blue Dog. My favorite thing to do
Is spinning circles. I went to school.
I go to school. I will go to school.
I was born in Denmark twenty-four years ago.
It was an easy birth. I do not cause trouble.
I do not make things difficult for others.
I have no family; they have vanished, one by one,
Until I am here alone with other members of my school.
I am healthy, but sometimes exhausted
From spinning circles. I sleep on a mat
Placed on the floor. My room is austere—abstract
Paintings on the walls in pastel colors—minimal
Furnishings placed close to the ground. My regret
Is that I have harmed myself from shame and have
            stopped

Dancing in the manner that I was trained.
I feel disappointment most often, more than any other
    emotion.)

All such aspects of the search yield
Rations for the choice. Spent from the efforts
Of stockpiling stray finds from our evening encounters,
We swim at night, moonlight spilling through water
As we regain our strength in the tepid warmth
Lifting us from the earth in a momentary gesture
Of embrace. Something comes to stay, then leaves
With a chilly draft sending shivers round your heart.
Sleepy daze as deliberation turns to frame
The velvet slipping evening air, releasing
Some infinitely disturbing immobility,
Trimmed in bleeding shades of all that comes to press
The meaning from our task. We'll have milk and crackers
For supper tonight. Place something on the table
Where things belong together with themselves,
As geese fly in coherent, then divergent patterns
Before disappearing past what it is we need to see.

Something awakens in the body, right above
Your head on the shelf where all thoughts linger
Awaiting incarnation, tentative possibilities
Promised some future hearing in the lottery of chance.
The dust removed, brushed away in a swift gesture
Of impatience—now that the time has come
The waiting is intolerable—the dust removed,
You pull the inventory from the stockpile of utility.
Closing your eyes now, you take the thought down
From the shelf above your head and begin to caress
The form as though it were a soft feminine breast
Erect with interest, hungry to feed desire.
The archive has collected interest, found its angle of
    repose.
Still, you are strangers negotiating intimacy.

Again the sky is empty of the congregation
We imagine has come only for our sake, as the horizon
Breaks to allow some other exit or admission.

First you awaken and then you die. The crime
Is letting go, forgetting how the stars broke through
One dark impenetrable night, seared the blanket
Overhead. Rumors of things to come
Had circulated through the air, brought news
That held you captive to what may yet put forward
A unified explanation. Searching for a witness,
The pilgrimage was under way. A message came,
Deserted scenes were left behind, filling with silence
Where cities will grow around their gossiping sleep.
A sea gull came following, mirrored by the sea
Stained with a darker memory of dawn. Early morning
Fog caressed the lips of the cliff, eroding any sense
Of where land ended and pure airy space began.

from *Denver Quarterly*

The Victor Vanquished

◊ ◊ ◊

for Tom, 1989

At the going rate, your body gave you
—made you—too much pain for you to call it
yours. Oh not the pain, the pain was all yours

and all you had; by the end you hugged it
closer than their anodine substitutes:
pain was your one religion, pain was bliss.

But this body, where almost everything hurt
and what didn't hurt didn't work—*yours*? Never!
Like anybody's, it gave nothing up

that soap and water couldn't wash away.
Whose was it then, this desecrated pond
where all fish die, where only scum persists?

Anybody's. Nobody's. Like a king
who keeps recognizing as "my people"
the rebels who have pulled him off the throne . . .

Your body not your body. What about
"your" friends? We want playmates we can own.
Could these be yours? Since every friendship

grows from some furtive apotheosis
of oneself, who were these dim intruders
presuming they inhabited your pain,

as if there could be room for them as well?
You would not have it—let them all go hang!
For two years, the body alone with its pain

suspended friendship like the rope that holds
a hanged man. All you wanted was to drop
this burden, even if it meant that you

would be the burden dropped. And "your" lovers?
What about love—was it like "your" disease,
an abnormal state of recognition

occurring in a normal man? Love is
not love until it is vulnerable—
then you were in it: up to here in love!

The verdict of their small-claims court: it takes
all kinds to make a sex. Had you made yours?
Everything is possible but not

everything is permitted: in love
you were a shadow pursuing shadows,
yet the habit of the chase enthralled you,

and you could not desist. You would make love
by listening, as women do. And by lying
still, alone, waiting. You did not wait long.

Life in general is, or ought to be,
as Crusoe said, one universal Act
of Solitude. You made it death as well.

from *Antæus*

Perfection and Derangement

◇ ◇ ◇

Dirt road, down a slope. In spring the trees are spackled with white blossoms, some flecks of pink. The branches look like long bones; the white has returned to them in the form of snow. Pinker berries dot the thinnest branches and thorns, and a spray of same lies across the rotted porch. If you look through the boarded-up windows you will see a contraption for restraining someone too sad to move.

Where can I rest? Satellites circle this snow-covered flatland. Orchards are bare by the reservoir, the green benches bent from cold. Under the ice I can see a leaf, a can, a tire, a fish, something from outer space. Then the water hardens like gelatin, swollen into lumps where old leaves are inlaid. An interior, destroyed by mismanagement.

Suffering is how the world informs the human mind that it is there. Suffering proves to the mind that it is exposed to alien substance, like it or not. If you can't act even while you suffer, you can only suffer and sink. Nonetheless a person has a right to protest and complain and to yearn bitterly for release.

May for one rejects any absolute dualism. She has it that past, present and future exist simultaneously. All time is the ONE's creation. Then police from Rhode Island call and want to know her status. They say they found her walking along the highway in shirtsleeves with no money, on her way to New York. They have brought her to the Cranston Medical Center and she can be picked up there.

Women are like roaches, they survive so much. They seem to grow tougher with each succeeding generation. I think the evolution of material things came before the entrance of women onto this earth, but they followed almost immediately. The first one was last seen through a hole in the clouds, going down through the top. A kind of intergalactic storm reviewer, she jumped directly for the heart and support.

Where are you that you don't invite me in, turning your hand out and over? Do you know which room I inhabit, the bed among beds and under stone joinings? That none of these belong to me?

To confabulate is to conceal your mental retardation. To confabulate is to be a fool filling in the gaps in your memory with detailed accounts of false events.

What do you dream about in the facility? Will you ever wake up to the facts and this way give up HOPE?

Your hands, like ten virtues, can only do so much. I have noticed, since coming here, that each person in this world is chasing his or her self at all times. Some people just move slower getting from the past person to the present or first one. Those who wail they want to go home are referring to a community where justice prevails and they get their mail. Though they are certainly sociopathic, they're not in prison, are they? They were never violent, but more likely terrified. Look into their oceanized eyes.

Our primordial metaphysical and religious experience begins in terror. This produces a modesty whose secret is only revealed through certain sacraments and only to those participating in them. This transaction is called THE DISCIPLINE OF THE SECRET.

I had just figured out how to live correctly when I realized it was too late, I had taken too long figuring it out.

Before on-rushing time I experience total helplessness. Like the words, "You shall see my back but my face shall not be seen," the loneliness in a human face belongs to the ONE.

Likewise for every one fact there's a second one to counter it. If therefore I knew all the facts, I would be paralysed—on wheels again at last.

The hidden countenance is one countenance worth contemplating. There a felicitous light swells into substance which sees as you see and breathes as you breathe; it even kisses where you kiss. Whisper your prayers if you want to call it out of the dark.

You asked me what I know about G-d and coincidence. I walk through you to tell you, the place where you stood like an opening in the form of an offering.

The soul originates in fire, cooperative and quick. It deteriorates into a self by becoming stiff and slow-moving. Now a place becomes a space suitable only for walking and the self often trails behind the body like a shadow. Better to feel your soul is rushing ahead of you than that your self is limping behind.

Colors return and scandalize the objects that were happily hidden. My position has changed. I've moved back to make room for the whole view, but still it's from that corner I see the space that held you.

I have failed to view my actions as having any importance, have spread myself thinly across the tops of things. I have resisted change, a new way of doing or thinking about the world. I have not lived up to the hopes anyone had for me. It makes me sick.

It's true that May had escaped in the morning and was returned by guards in the afternoon, saying *Because I had nowhere to go.* Now she is just sitting down in a dazed state. Inappropriate laughter as usual. She was very upset about the commitment proceedings. Her sister really hates her.

Why all the emphasis on lobbies, Paul asked me. I told him that they can be shortcuts to streets. I didn't want him to know that every lobby is private, so the homeless have one less place to congregate. The Department of Mental Health should have a terraced waterfall cascading down the stairs to show visitors how it feels being scared.

Come here and fill the space waiting.
May I lick your lips?
Any opinion on the defense budget?
Come here, never. You can rest there in the open door.
Three songs—refrigerator, birds and a trolley start at 5 a.m.

Bend to get the hint: there have been advances in cruelty since Oliver Twist.

Poor Paul called the sky Tubby. Snow, Tubby, he would say.

Anyone ordering restraints in this place has got to be familiar with the way it feels on the other side. I carry a little glass ball on a thread as my refuge and my joy. I do the lights, or did, every year on the facility green. I put the spotlight on dogs. It was often foggy in December. And I bet Christmas Eve wouldn't have eaten that apple if it had been that foggy. She wouldn't have been able to see it in the first place.

What will you give me to leave you since I haven't begun to die yet? I'm sorry. My mother would always say, "You get more excited by Christmas than any child I know." That showed how much she loved me before she left me in Valley Forget. We had a duplex with all the amenities, including hardwood floors, central air conditioning, fireplace, private roof deck, a Euro-style kitchen and a ranch-style livingroom. It was amazing. Ma kept a table set and waiting all day every day. When I had time I'd grab a hot dog and cola and sit right down in front of a display of china and silver. No matter if I wolfed down my lunch. I appreciated every bite in that environment.

Tonight the ward is quiet. People have a zombie attitude and seem only inwardly hostile. Sam oiled his hair with toothpaste before bed. I had seven vacancies and fourteen beds. Some of these people are ready for another redeemer, I tell you. Every event is packed with hidden meaning.

I said we won't accept a lenient sentence since evil is built into our system. Sustained, said Your Honor. I can't help worrying, though, we're so broke. No awnings, no boat hulls or sails, no automobile panels, no water skis, no beverage bottle carriers, no covers for cushions or appliance handles, to name just a few.

No family, no friends.
In the shelter hot meals are liable to clang. Eyes are like primitive telescopes facing the sea. I've been in that trick fortress too long. Someone is always fucking following me. There's no safety.

May is now acting very strangely, staring at the ceiling rigidly, tongue in cheek. She saw two red nails in a door that gave her a sign of Christ. Later when she was staring at the ceiling she said the holes in it looked as though they were breathing!

Now the snow is going up and down, now it is waving to the side. The branches seem to lift into zebra-snakes asking for food from the cloaked fir trees. The sky is solid white. A full moon will be rising, pink, and close to the horizon soon, and will polish the night shapes.

What was lost, comes back—like May—but how do we know we are not already somebody's tomorrow? Am I here and waiting, the table set and the toast warm for someone alive in a yesterday?

I was kicked out of Ma's apartment a month after she left, so I don't know if she came home again. She left me a note beginning, *Dear Reality,* and signed, *Love, Me.* The man who kicked me out of the apartment was so greedy I bet he would appraise the value of a walnut shell if an ant wanted to live there.

Is G-d a place that it should move with me in my car? Or is this ability to move a sign that it's not a place at all? The ONE experiences itself through its creation, even though it existed before and beyond that creation, I'm told. The ONE is lonely and loves voices that call to it, even when it can do nothing to help but only sympathize.

Likewise the soul informs the body of its presence but doesn't really have an effect on acts.

Stop feeling sorry for May when she's put in seclusion. At 7 a.m. she assaulted poor Sam in his wheelchair, hitting him with her fist several times on the back of the head. When the nurse came with meds to her room, she threw them back at her and became assaultive again. Was given 100 mg. of thorazine and was quiet for the rest of the night. If you feel sorry for her it's like saying that G-d has abandoned her. Imagine how that makes her feel. Just try to help her out instead.

It's all very well for you to say you don't know G-d, but what would you say if you learned that G-d doesn't know YOU?

May said, I lost my self-control. It just got away from me. Later it came out as a splash of color here, twelve smears of gray there, oak trees shot in morbid details, the hum of a cello, words overheard and a pirouette. I think that each one now is the signature of a lost person looking for a home—not a shelter—a home like the one that was promised to us somewhere along the line.

from *O.blek*

On the Bearing of Waitresses

◇　◇　◇

Always I thought they suffered, the way they huffed
through the Benzedrine light of waffle houses,
hustling trays of omelettes, gossiping by the grill,
or pruning passes like the too prodigal buds of roses,
and I imagined each come home to a trailer court,
the yard of bricked-in violets, the younger sister
pregnant and petulant at her manicure, the mother
with her white Bible, the father sullen in his corner.
Wasn't that the code they telegraphed in smirks?
And wasn't this disgrace, to be public and obliged,
observed like germs or despots about to be debunked?
Unlikely brides, apostles in the gospel of stereotypes,
their future was out there beyond the parked trucks,
between the beer joints and the sexless church,
the images we'd learned from hayseed troubadours—
perfume, grease, and the rending of polarizing loves.
But here in the men's place, they preserved a faint
decorum of women and, when they had shuffled past us,
settled in that realm where the brain approximates
names and rounds off the figures under uniforms.
Not to be honored or despised, but to walk as spies would,
with almost alien poise in the imperium of our disregard,
to go on steadily, even on the night of the miscarriage,
to glide, quick smile, at the periphery of appetite.
And always I had seen them listening, as time brought
and sent them, hovering and pivoting as the late
orders turned strange, *blue garden, brown wave*. Spit

in the salad, wet socks wrung into soup, and this happened.
One Sunday morning in a truckstop in Bristol, Virginia,
a rouged and pancaked half-Filipino waitress
with hair dyed the color of puffed wheat and mulberries
singled me out of the crowd of would-be bikers
and drunken husbands guzzling coffee to sober up
in time to cart their disgusted wives and children
down the long street to the First Methodist Church.
Because I had a face she trusted, she had me wait
that last tatter of unlawful night that hung there
and hung there like some cast-off underthing
caught on the spikes of a cemetery's wrought-iron fence.
And what I had waited for was no charm of flesh,
not the hard seasoning of luck, or work, or desire,
but all morning, in the sericea by the filthy city lake,
I suffered her frightened lie, how she was wanted
in Washington by the CIA, in Vegas by the FBI—
while time shook us like locks that would not break.
And I did not speak, though she kept pausing to look
back across one shoulder, as though she were needed
in the trees, but waxing her slow paragraphs into
chapters, filing the air with her glamour and her shame.

from *Transparent Gestures*

When One Has Lived a Long Time Alone

◇   ◇   ◇

1

When one has lived a long time alone,
one refrains from swatting the fly
and lets him go, and one hesitates to strike
the mosquito, though more than willing to slap
the flesh under her, and one lifts the toad
from the pit too deep for him to hop out of
and carries him to the grass, without minding
the toxic urine he slicks his body with,
and one envelops, in a towel, the swift
who fell down the chimney and knocks herself
against the window glass and releases her outside
and watches her fly free, a life line flung at reality,
when one has lived a long time alone.

2

When one has lived a long time alone,
one grabs the snake behind the head
and holds him until he stops trying to stick
the orange tongue, which splits at the end
into two black filaments and jumps out
like a fire-eater's belches and has little

in common with the pimpled pink lump that shapes
sounds and sleeps inside the human mouth,
into one's flesh, and clamps it between his jaws,
letting the gaudy tips show, as children do
when concentrating, and as very likely
one does oneself, without knowing it,
when one has lived a long time alone.

3

When one has lived a long time alone,
among regrets so immense the past occupies
nearly all the room there is in consciousness,
one notices in the snake's eyes, which look back
without paying less attention to the future,
the first coating of the opaque milky-blue
leucoma snakes get when about to throw
their skins and become new—meanwhile continuing,
of course, to grow old—the exact *bleu passé*
that discolors the corneas of the blue-eyed
when they lie back at last and look for heaven,
a blurring one can see means they will never find it,
when one has lived a long time alone.

4

When one has lived a long time alone,
one holds the snake near a loudspeaker disgorging
gorgeous sound and watches him crook
his forepart into four right angles
as though trying to slow down the music
flowing through him, in order to absorb it
like milk of paradise into the flesh,
and now a glimmering appears at his mouth,
such a drop of intense fluid as, among humans,
could form after long exciting at the tip

of the penis, and as he straightens himself out
he has the pathos one finds in the penis,
when one has lived a long time alone.

5

When one has lived a long time alone,
one can fall to poring upon a creature,
contrasting its eternity's-face to one's own
full of hours, taking note of each difference,
exaggerating it, making it everything,
until the other is utterly other, and then,
with hard effort, possibly with tongue sticking out,
going back over each one once again
and cancelling it, seeing nothing now
but likeness, until . . . half an hour later
one starts awake, taken aback at how eagerly
one swoons into the happiness of kinship,
when one has lived a long time alone.

6

When one has lived a long time alone
and listens at morning to mourning doves
sound their *kyrie eleision,* or the small thing
spiritualizing onto one's shoulder cry "pewit-phoebe!"
or peabody-sparrows at midday send schoolboys'
whistlings across the field, or at dusk, undamped,
unforgiving clinks, as from stonemasons' chisels,
or on trees' backs tree frogs scratch the thighs'
needfire awake, or from the frog pond pond frogs
raise their *ave verum corpus*—listens to those
who hop or fly call down upon us the mercy
of other tongues—one hears them as inner voices,
when one has lived a long time alone.

7

When one has lived a long time alone,
one knows only consciousness consummates,
and as the conscious one among these others
uttering compulsory cries of being here—
the least flycatcher witching up "che-bec,"
or redheaded woodpecker clanging out his
music from a metal drainpipe, or ruffed grouse
drumming "thrump thrump thrump thrump-thrump-
thrump-thrump-rup-rup-rup-rup-rup-r-r-r-r-r-r"
through the trees, all of them in time's
unfolding trying to cry themselves into self-knowing—
one knows one is here to hear them into shining,
when one has lived a long time alone.

8

When one has lived a long time alone,
one likes alike the pig, who brooks no deferment
of gratification, and the porcupine, or thorned pig,
who enters the cellar but not the house itself
because of eating down the cellar stairs on the way up,
and one likes the worm, who by bunching herself together
and expanding rubs her way through the ground,
no less than the butterfly, who totters full of worry
among the day-lilies, as they darken,
and more and more one finds one likes
any other species better than one's own,
which has gone amok, making one self-estranged,
when one has lived a long time alone.

9

When one has lived a long time alone,
sour, misanthropic, one fits to one's defiance
the satanic boast—*It is better to reign*

in hell than to submit on earth—
and forgets one's kind, as does the snake,
who has stopped trying to escape and moves
at ease across one's body, slumping into its contours,
adopting its temperature, and abandons hope
of the sweetness of friendship or love
—before long can barely remember what they are—
and covets the stillness in inorganic matter,
in a self-dissolution one may not know how to halt,
when one has lived a long time alone.

10

When one has lived a long time alone,
and the hermit thrush calls and there is an answer,
and the bullfrog, head half out of water, remembers
the exact sexual cantillations of his first spring,
and the snake slides over the threshold and disappears
among the stones, one sees they all live
to mate with their kind, and one knows,
after a long time of solitude, after the many steps taken
away from one's kind, toward the kingdom of strangers,
the hard prayer inside one's own singing
is to come back, if one can, to one's own,
a world almost lost, in the exile that deepens,
when one has lived a long time alone.

11

When one has lived a long time alone,
one wants to live again among men and women,
to return to that place where one's ties with the human
broke, where the disquiet of death and now
also of history glimmers its firelight on faces,
where the gaze of the new baby looks past the gaze
of the great-granny, and where lovers speak,
on lips blowsy from kissing, that language

the same in each mouth, and like birds at daybreak
blether the song that is both earth's and heaven's,
until the sun has risen, and they stand
in a halo of being united: kingdom come,
when one has lived a long time alone.

from *The Atlantic Monthly*

Gangue

◇ ◇ ◇

When the floors, the walls, the windows in
This room shake, it could mean the train,
The earthquake, the neighbors. Plaster is
The last up, first to fall, having cracked from
Ceiling to baseboard. Then it is patched, painted to
Match. In the curtain at the opera is an opening the actors
Walk through for applause. They come out, they go
Back in. The orchestra stands and we see a sea
Of heads. The playing was loud enough, the singing
Was loud enough, too. If there is confusion
Later, in the parking garage among cars, cars
Must have their own time. They speed home, tires on
Smooth road, half the clocks on the dashes working.
I've walked the hypotenuse of the trapezoid piazza in
Pienza. There is no space left in Siena's Duomo to
Carve one's initials, the floor already completely
Covered with graffiti. I've thrown confetti *con brio*.
I've clapped at flocks of pigeons flapping around
Towers. I've waxed the tile floor until the squares
Became diamonds. I've preferred tree houses over non-
Tree houses. The brush fire out of control has been
Contained. If time is a stoppered bottle, I am
A bucket. The camera clicks and goes on to the next
Picture. I've lived, mostly, in wood-frame houses,
Except for one stone farmhouse. And one root
Cellar for one summer. Renting from a landlord
Seems feudal and is only missing a little machicolation

Or a moat. The suicide note so-and-so left
In the car had some great lines. In the paint
Factory, all the paint was red.
The doctor threw his patient's vocal cords in the dumpster.
The earthquake increased the size of his property.
There was a fissure all down his throat.
We have words like crack, buzz, and ring,
And cracked, buzzed, and rang. These are noises
That disappear when I cover my ears.

from *The Gettysburg Review*

Facing It

◇ ◇ ◇

My black face fades,
hiding inside the black granite.
I said I wouldn't,
dammit: No tears.
I'm stone. I'm flesh.
My clouded reflection eyes me
like a bird of prey, the profile of night
slanted against morning. I turn
this way—the stone lets me go.
I turn that way—I'm inside
the Vietnam Veterans Memorial
again, depending on the light
to make a difference.
I go down the 58,022 names,
half-expecting to find
my own in letters like smoke.
I touch the name Andrew Johnson;
I see the booby trap's white flash.
Names shimmer on a woman's blouse
but when she walks away
the names stay on the wall.
Brushstrokes flash, a red bird's
wings cutting across my stare.
The sky. A plane in the sky.
A white vet's image floats
closer to me, then his pale eyes
look through mine. I'm a window.

He's lost his right arm
inside the stone. In the black mirror
a woman's trying to erase names:
No, she's brushing a boy's hair.

from *Dien Cai Dau*

Ikon: The Harrowing of Hell

◊ ◊ ◊

Down through the tomb's inward arch
He has shouldered out into Limbo
to gather them, dazed, from dreamless slumber:
the merciful dead, the prophets,
the innocents just His own age and those
unnumbered others waiting here
unaware, in an endless void He is ending
now, stooping to tug at their hands,
to pull them from their sarcophagi,
dazzled, almost unwilling. Didmas,
neighbor in death, Golgotha dust
still streaked on the dried sweat of his body
no one had washed and anointed, is here,
for sequence is not known in Limbo;
the promise, given from cross to cross
at noon, arches beyond sunset and dawn.
All these He will swiftly lead
to the Paradise road: they are safe.
That done, there must take place that struggle
no human presumes to picture:
living, dying, descending to rescue the just
from shadow, were lesser travails
than this: to break
through earth and stone of the faithless world
back to the cold sepulchre, tearstained
stifling shroud: to break from *them*
back into breath and heartbeat, and walk

the world again, closed into days and weeks again,
wounds of His anguish open, and Spirit
streaming through every cell of flesh
so that if mortal sight could bear
to perceive it, it would be seen
His mortal flesh was lit from within, now,
and aching for home. He must return,
first, in Divine patience, and know
hunger again, and give
to humble friends the joy
of giving Him food—fish and a honeycomb.

from *American Poetry Review*

Scouting

◇ ◇ ◇

I'm the man who gets off the bus
at the bare junction of nothing
with nothing, and then heads back
to where we've been as though
the future were stashed somewhere
in that tangle of events we call
"Where I come from." Where I
came from the fences ran right
down to the road, and the lone woman
leaning back on her front porch as she
quietly smoked asked me what did
I want. Confused as always, I
answered, "Water," and she came to me
with a frosted bottle and a cup,
shook my hand, and said, "Good luck."
That was forty years ago, you say,
when anything was possible. No,
it was yesterday, the gray icebox
sat on the front porch, the crop
was tobacco and not yet in, you
could hear it sighing out back.
The rocker gradually slowed as
she came toward me but never
stopped and the two of us went on
living in time. One of her eyes
had a pale cast and looked nowhere
or into the future where without

regrets she would give up the power
to grant life, and I would darken
like wood left in the rain and then
fade into only a hint of the grain.
I went higher up the mountain
until my breath came in gasps,
my sight darkened, and I slept
to the side of the road to waken
chilled in the sudden July cold,
alone and well. What is it like
to come to, nowhere, in darkness,
not knowing who you are, not
caring if the wind calms, the stars
stall in their sudden orbits,
the cities below go on without
you, screaming and singing?
I don't have the answer. I'm
scouting, getting the feel
of the land, the way the fields
step down the mountainsides
hugging their battered, sagging
wire fences to themselves as though
both day and night they needed
to know their limits. Almost still,
the silent dogs wound into sleep,
the gray cabins breathing steadily
in moonlight, tomorrow wakening
slowly in the clumps of mountain oak
and pine where streams once ran
down the little white rock gullies.
You can feel the whole country
wanting to waken into a child's dream,
you can feel the moment reaching
back to contain your life and forward
to whatever the dawn brings you to.
In the dark you can love this place.

from *Western Humanities Review*

Time

◇ ◇ ◇

I have a friend whose hair is like time: dark
deranged coils lit by a lamp
when she bends back her head to laugh. A unique event,
such as the crucifixion of Christ, was not
subject to repetition, thought St. Augustine, and therefore,
time is linear. Does the universe
have an end, a beginning? Yes, the former the door
through which she departs, the latter
the door by which she returns,
and inbetween there is no rest from wanting her.

Time—each moment of which a hair on a child's nape.
Time—the chain between the churning tractor and the stump.
Time—her gown tossed like a continent at the creation.
Newton, an absolutist, thought time a container
in which the universe exists—nonending, nonbeginning.
Time—enamored, forgiven by dust
and capable of calling a single blade of grass an oasis.
Time—of swivel, small streams, plinth, stanchions.
And then Kant says, no, time does not apply
to the universe, only to the way we think about time.

Time—the spot where the violin touches the maestro's cheek.
Time—an endless range of cumulonimbus.
Time—Good Monarch of the deepest blue inevitable.
The relativists (with whom the absolutists,
as usual, disagree) argue that concepts of past,

present, and future are mind dependent, i.e.,
would time exist without conscious beings?
Oh Ultimate Abstract, is there time
in time, is there rest, in time,
from wanting her?

from *American Poetry Review*

Slipped Quadrant

◊ ◊ ◊

As if by late light shaped of its
arrival,   echoed announcement
      come from afar,   loosed
      allure,   the as-if of it its
         least appeasable part.
                              Rich
      tense within we called it,
         would without end,   seed
   within a seed sown elsewhere,
                                   somewhere
         said to've been known as
Ttha.
            Wrought   surfaces, putative
      soul,   cheated heart.   Shot
         body borne up to be looked
      at, learned from, one
                        heretical
moment's reprimand . . .
                           Something a
      Sufi said in Andalusia.
                        Something
         said to've been said before.
   Ominous music made a mumblers
                                 academy,
      vatic scat,   to be alive
   was to be warned it said . . .

                    And of
    loss long assured of its
        occurrence,   echoed
agreement grown more remote,
                            long out of
        reach,   not as yet known by
    name though not nameless,
                                    swift,
uninterpretable design . . .
                        In oblique
    league with majesty,   secret,
unannounced,   came to where the
    flutes of the Afar spat salt,
                            limbs
under loosefitting cloth . . .
        Came then to within a stone's
    throw of Ttha,   very far,
        weary, felt we'd walked with
                                    weights
    on our feet.
            Saw the in we sought
    ran on, some said stop, some
        we'd barely started.
                    Stood us
    up within sight of Ttha, strewn
    kin, sat us down sipping hog's-hoof
                            tea . . .

Trashed ecstasy. Impudent if.
                    Said
what but wind on our stomachs fed
    it, whim. Felt for it falling away
    from it, called it "Calling it the
                            earth,"
    unsprung.   Shied away might worry
cease, drew near, bud bursting out
out of earshot, wind out of India,
    three-digit heat.   Scratched
                        air

screamed reparation, strung spillages
  fingers pried apart as they
                    struck . . .
Running start without which no escape, with-
out Rasta's far-eye squint   not
                        see . . .

     Numbed comfort.   Lungless bellower.
Believed it.   Faith gotten back,
                      as if not,
  broke in on its answer, made its caught
mouth twitch . . .   Grew numb,   having
  nothing to say, said so.   Glum,
  though if need be not.   Encephalic
                    blow.
Hollow emblem.   Blocked.
                   Heads wet,
  many a midnight soaking. Slogan-weary
  sleepers. Dream of a just world.
Saw the in we sought ran deep, sat us
  down with chills, polyrhythmic
                  shivers . . .
Pinched earth, outrun by longing.
  Whimsical inlet.   Renegade
               wish

from *Avec*

Road

◇ ◇ ◇

1

comfort notions
   correction
incapable of keeping
   case-histories

foresee requisites
   talk about
a grinning idiot

   (closed down
nothing comes up
they ram a car
   up there
instead of a cop)

". . . necessary to remember
Marat and Danton, Saint-Just and Babeuf . . ."

2

A long line came to me in my sleep
   impulse weak
a drain
   a leak

faces change
'turnover'
on the shopfloor
payday to payday
  accommodation
Banks, don't they
  make you
the make, on the make
  no word for
the Banker's benign
  paternal
smile: the small
  transfers
appease—what—sure, only
  more new
  more new
paltry and a name
"Did I do something?"
"What did I do?"
Sorry, baby,
I'm clumsy
You think I don't
know I'm a, uh,
(Allegory of the wage-slave
his awe and his lack
  of access)
Dante: You are my master and my author
Virgil: This cowardice, this sleep-in-the-
  heart you harbor

3

Won't reach your hands
  until Monday
your eyes until Tuesday, maybe,
you are a man who has
  influence?

Construed as forward, or,
worse, aggressive,
a clerk in an office

Boxcar forklife meathook
dock (south dock) truck
   shopfloor
foreman bays (boys)
shopfloor forklift foreman
   2200 pcs
   50 lb ea
44 pcs per pallet
chimney-stack
Saturday morning
scafe = plum(b)-with-the-world
   a carpenter's term
exact or perfect
   circled
even with jubilant
   what word to say
brought-to-bear

4

"Your hands, look what's happening
   to your hands"
"You don't fall asleep anymore
   you pass out"
He in bed and she beside
   to rub the lotion
in. "This will help them"
   she said, softly, a lullaby
maybe. "I brought this
   to help your hands"
(Rations, in wartime,
   patrimony,
home, to put it firmly)

He would tell the foreman
'I want to go to war'
   need Friday off
   maybe Monday
look at it this way
if you and the crew
if you and the crew
   against
like guys from the Harvard Business School
"Listen, Tony, if the Party could pay you
   Navy pay"
But to go and have nothing to say
He would write her that on a card
"?!," just that, then would she know
the gentleman in a carriage
   his gold coins
lost, in a meadow,
and the oh, so obedient boy
   who found them for him

                              5

"as such"

and then "program"
and then "pogrom"

the joke about Jews was
(who has been disappeared)

         clouds burst
            strong rain
         hardly apocalyptic
         thunder and lightning
            all the same

ungenerous . selfish . mean(hearted) . unclean

shank shoulder cheekmeat
slunk

mean amid astonish-
ment

lift   lift   lift   lift

stack   stack   stack   stack

(wait)   (wait)   (wait)   (wait)

the forklifts load and unload the racks
the forklifts load and unload the racks

the forklifts load and unload the racks

the forklifts load and unload the racks

6

To demand the time of day

The demand of the time of day

To demonstrate (for others) the taking of

Vows

To perform vows

Resolution/Resolve

A parable of Rebellion

The coward (Sir Kay)

Misery is Repetition

We was robbed

7

worker 1: "we used to
                sit in the
                pickup in high
                school and slam
                whiskey down
                before philosophy"
worker 2: "what kind
                was it?"
worker 1: "of whiskey?"
worker 2: "of philosophy"
worker 1: "Descartes
                and who was
                the other
                bozo . . ."
worker 2: "Kant and
                Wittgenstein
                now that's
                heavy shit"
worker 1: "you have to
                get fucked
                up to do
                that shit"

worker 3: "you ever fucking have to
                stand in a picket-line?!"
                "you ever fucking have to
                punch out a scab?!"

Highway parallel to the rails
in route
   to the city by the sea
I heard the man on the train
   describe
the man with the family and camper
He said: *factory slave*
He said: "look at him, off on his
   two week slice of the year"
His piece of the pie, I guess,
   the figure of speech
The man on the train's
   cheap suit
wrinkled from sleeping in it
who could afford to speak
superior, drinking the money
   he saved
taking a train
in place of a plane

(and I say I
under the sign of
the shift in address
from the group or party 'we'
to the accusative 'you'
—the attack in the Manifesto—
"this person must be swept out of the way,
   and made impossible")

9

We are at a conference that features yet another
   released Russian
prisoner of 'the system'

We were loose some even naked and dancing
He told me to leave
    and then his friend said leave

No picture available of the dream

A man and a woman
    the woman
or by association
    his class
her word was *stupid*
he shouted NO

The length of the O
intonation/duration
at the end of the O
    this poverty
    this prison

(the gold-bearded ensign
didn't have his pants on)

One group at a table to listen to
    yet another released Russian Jew
another group dances like wild

10

Value
trans (what do
you say

system
know better
than who

pull away   trade)

did all
who was

step imprint

11

No man may come
   trewthe to
but he syng
   si dedero
Speke, spende and spede
   quoth Jon of Bathon
and therefore synne
fareth as wilde
flode, trew love
   is away
that was so gode
   God do bote
for now is tyme
for now is tyme
   to be war

12

He said: "We have no concept of combat"
He said: "You will go to jail
   if you lead the workers well"
"A quarter-century of caution
   to be on their side
   to be by their side
to move with real struggles
   necessary to move
in the unions, in the union
movement, to be communist"

O word not the same word
  as the word
when the word was a new word
was there an original word
  logos, or legend
the red flag and the rider
in a Paris square

Stamped with the birthmarks
  out of whose womb
They said the state would wither away
  party and politics disappear
Each according to their ability
Each according to their needs
  that labor cease to be mere means
Experience help to show
  the first experience, the early years
Lenin opened the congress by saying
He said: We have opened the road

13

Victory the protective deity
in Pindar, episodes from heroic legend
the beginning: invocation (vocation)
Transport and delivery, turned upside down
upheaval
not individual, not caprice
like a fad under cover of outcry
Why, instead of 200–400 lines, don't you
  write 20 or even 10 lines?
"He waits forever for the stroke in his head
  and is divided"
"The great adventure never accepts one without
  strength"

Nobody's to be blamed for being born a slave.
Pottier was born into poverty, and all his life
    remained a working man,
winning a living first as a packer and later by tracing
    patterns on cloth.
No, he is an artist, and nothing more, a stranger
    to the Party.
If some of the *cadre*, who work beside the people,
    sat down to describe—

Husk work, the wording
heart cannot make up
    fantasy-
land look out on the land
the 'time' longed for
like a room lit with tallow candles
    long ago
where the union held their meeting while
the unemployed rioted at the charity ball

Party-colored flowers, a complete encyclopedia
philosophy, religion, art, politics, progaganda
the Birons and Arakcheyevs, carnival travellers,
    gamblers, scoundrels, pimps
alongside, as always, the amiable Manilovs
their charlatan phrases, benevolent visions
florid restored the shattered throne and applauded
history steeped in vomit
middle-class claptrap and the crown's demands

    Summon hum human hymn him
        dexterity
    manual dexterity
    4A7. (maple leaf) .2X3,
        83 or S3

The speed of the Beast the speed of
   the spoken word
a slack jaw and a stirrup
what hopes to find a heart inside, like in a
   lady's locket
the composite, the legible figure, the round
shape the syllable forces the mouth to make

      Chorus (proletarian,
        promethean):
      'We have not reached the end
        of history'
      'We have not come to the end
        of human time'

14

A land under labor, wells, access to meadows
Belongs to the hammer blows, in arena of wrest
Phalanx of heroes
Heft, like Remus and Romulus
The ruck, or song
Streets, city strata, throne and throng
Was it his fault or his misfortune?
(You, the son of a father murdered in Bezdna
And you, the father of a youth murdered in Penza)
Humble is as Humble does, cannot explain away

Ago the lolling, law-abiding boy
He went away to war
Village collapsed, never to be restored
And then: the steam-engine, the spinning machine
   and the power-loom
In the classical factory
One man no longer made one thing
Collar rod couple hook shunt anvil Spring

Town-bond
Building under command of the campaign's 1-2-3
Mister Coupon struck up a workers' song

from *Hambone*

Afternoon of a McGrath

◇ ◇ ◇

For my son Tomasito McGrath
after a visit to McGrath, Minnesota
(Aitken County)
early winter '74–'75

This morning there was one McGrath in Aitken County.
                                                    Now
There are three: the town, Tomasito, and myself.
                              And at this rate of growth
The County will remain alive at least ten minutes longer,
Though the town is disappearing: fast: in a thickening snow:
Which is also the snow of time, the secret invisible snow
That falls in summer and falls in the fall and in spring: the snow
We are all disappearing into—all but Tomasito
Who has found a god-dog to mush home with if he knew where
     that was.

This town, which carries our name into the rising night,
Is one of those lost places in which I have found myself
Often . . . though they always had other names—and sometimes
     I did.
What could I expect to find in a place where the lakes hold only
Private water? A walk or a wake away from the Dead
Sea of Mille Lacs where all class-struggle is ethnic?
                                                    Place
Where each grave plot is bespoke and the loudest talk is on
     tombstones?

Did I think to push open a gate and enter a century of sleep
Where only myself is awake? But that's just the world I live in
Outside the township limits . . .
                                    Perhaps I expected to find
Death McGrath, that stranger I meet so often in dreams,
The one I thought was myself disguised in the drag of death?
Perhaps he is one of these Indians, now in full retreat
(With their white comrades) from the shots and the double shots of
        General
Alcohol?
            But it's not the bargirl, inside whose head
It is snowing, as it snows in mine, and behind whose eyes I see
The slow turn to the left of those permanent low-pressure systems . . .
And that's McGrath. I will never forget it, now, Tomasito—
Our ghosts are here forever now because you were here
With this snow and this bar and that dog—see: what you have
        invented!
And so I will put this poem under a stone somewhere
On a road I will never walk on again, as I have done
Another time.
                Or put it with our hidden wishing stone
To remember us by "forever": now: as the town disappears
Into the blizzard . . .
                    and all the McGraths drift into
That snow, that permanent white where all our colors fade.

The night is closing down. But I'd like McGrath to continue
Beyond this winter and those to come—though THAT beyond
Is beyond all hope.
                So let me stop: here: then . . .
                                            —drifting

Into the universe and past all stars: toward those
Dark holes in space I must recognize as home.

from *The Nation*

Barbie's Ferrari

◊ ◊ ◊

Nothing is quite alien or quite recognizable at this speed,
Though there is the suggestion of curve, a mutant
Curvature designed, I suppose, to soften or offset
The stiletto toes and karate arms that were too
Angular for her last car, a Corvette as knifed as Barbie
Herself, and not the bloodred of Italian Renaissance.
This is Attention. This is detail fitted to sheer
Velocity. For her knees, after all, are locked—
Once fitted into the driving pit, she can only accelerate
Into a future that becomes hauntingly like the past:
Nancy Drew in her yellow roadster, a convertible,
I always imagined, the means to an end
Almost criminal in its freedom, its motherlessness.
For Barbie, too, is innocent of parents, pressing
Her unloved breasts to the masculine wheel, gunning
The turn into the hallway and out over the maiming stairs,
Every jolt slamming her uterus into uselessness, sealed,
Sealed up and preserved, everything about her becoming
Pure Abstraction and the vehicle for Desire: to be Nancy,
To be Barbie, to feel the heaven of Imagination
Breathe its ether on your cheeks, rosying in the slipstream
As the speedster/roadster/Ferrari plummets over the rail
Into the ocean of waxed hardwood below. To crash and burn
And be retrieved. To unriddle the crime. To be
Barbie with a plot! That's the soulful beauty of it.
That's the dreaming child.
Not the dawn of Capital, the factories of Hong Kong

Reversing the currency in Beijing. Not the ovarian
Moon in eclipse. Just the dreaming child, the orphan,
Turning in slow motion in the air above the bannister,
For whom ideas of gender and marketplace are nothings
Less than nothing. It's the car she was born for.
It's Barbie you mourn for.

from *American Poetry Review*

Concerning That Prayer
I Cannot Make

◇　◇　◇

Jesus, I am cruelly lonely
and I do not know what I have done
nor do I suspect that you will answer me.

And, what is more, I have spent
these bare months bargaining
with my soul as if I could make her
promise to love me when now it seems
that what I meant when I said "soul"
was that the river reflects
the railway bridge just as the sky
says it should—it speaks *that* language.

I do not know who you are.

I come here every day
to be beneath this bridge,
to sit beside this river,
so I *must* have seen the way
the clouds just slide
under the rusty arch—
without snagging on the bolts,
how they are borne along on the dark water—
I must have noticed their fluent speed
and also how that tattered blue T-shirt

remains snagged on the crown
of the mostly sunk dead tree
despite the current's constant pulling.
Yes, somewhere in my mind there must
be the image of a sky blue T-shirt, caught,
and the white islands of ice flying by
and the light clouds flying slowly
under the bridge, though today the river's
fully melted. I must have seen.

But I did not see.

I am not equal to my longing.
Somewhere there should be a place
the exact shape of my emptiness—
there should be a place
responsible for taking one back.
The river, of course, has no mercy—
it just lifts the dead fish
toward the sea.

Of course, of course.

What I *meant* when I said "soul"
was that there should be a place.

On the far bank the warehouse lights
blink red, then green, and all the yellow
machines with their rusted scoops and lifts
sit under a thin layer of sunny frost.

And look—
my own palm—
there, slowly rocking.
It is *my* pale palm—
palm where a black pebble
is turning and turning.

Listen—
all you bare trees
burrs
brambles
pile of twigs
red and green lights flashing
muddy bottle shards
shoe half buried—listen

listen, I am holy.

from *Virginia Quarterly Review*

Quatrains for Pegasus

◇ ◇ ◇

Breakfast over, to Memorial Park we'd go
On sunny Saturdays, I and Mrs McGrath.
We took care to approach the monument each time
By a new swamp-oak or palmetto-shaded path.

The paths converged at the heart of a parched fairway
Where Earth, not looking its best, rose out of the blue
Reflecting pool: Earth starved to a global ribcage,
Meridians of bronze—how the bare sky shone through!

Yet round it four horses of stone still fairly white
(Or just the one horse times four—with reflections, eight)
Held up the globe in a caracole that thrilled me,
Eager like them for the further, the ultimate

Thrill due on the stroke of ten. A black man in rags—
Making no secret of it as we looked his way—
Grasped something under the ground and gave it a turn.
The circulatory system brought into play

Filled the air with a magical diamond surf
Hoofs came plunging through, jets like fireworks rocketed
In four directions, as though from the horses' brows.
I wondered if passing through a white horse's head

Was curing the municipal water for good
Of its butts and tinfoil? Making trees toss with joy,
Flagstones glitter and steam? Would the process also
Help Mrs McGrath's bad hip, make me a good boy,

And keep—for each morning paper brought fresh horrors—
Our whole world from starving like the Armenians,
Its bones from coming to light like the Lindbergh baby's . . . ?
Mrs McGrath's young brother lay buried in France,

And these were questions—what if she knew the answers!—
I was too little and tactful to ask my nurse.
The more she said, the wickeder the world got.
Don't let it, I begged the horses, get any worse.

from *The Nation*

The Morning Train

◊ ◊ ◊

In the same way that the sea
becomes something else the moment we
are on it with its horizon all around
us and its weight
bearing us up so a journey seems not
to be one as long as we are

travelling but instead we
are awake sitting still at a bare
window that is familiar to us but not
in truth ours as
we know and facing us there is a line
of socks hanging in the sunlight

over a patch of onions
blue in their summer luminous rows
of carrots the youth of lettuces to be
glimpsed once only
dahlias facing along a white-painted
picket fence beside a plum tree

at the side of a station
like so many into which the green
revolving woods pointing fields brief moments of
rivers bridges
clusters of roofs again and again have
turned slowing first and repeating

their one gesture of approach
with a different name out of the place
of names a clock on which the hour changes
but not of course
the day arrangements of figures staring
through the last stages of waiting

only there is nothing on
the platform now but the morning light
the old gray door into the station is
standing open
in a silence through which the minute hand
overhead can be heard falling

while a hen is talking to
herself beyond the fence and why are
we not moving what are we waiting for now
only the hum
in our ears continuing to tell us
that we have been travelling since

whatever day it was that
city with its tower and there was
the night with its iron ceilings echoing
couplings through the
shunted hours in the all-night restaurant
between trains then the socks begin

to slip away on their line
the garden swings softly behind its
fence and in a few hours when we think we are
almost home at
last we will look up through the pane across
a stony field plowed since we left

rusting at noon and the same
flowers will be leaning on the south
wall of the house from which we have watched the trains

pass and we will
see clearly as we rush by all of its
empty windows filled with the sea

from *The New Yorker*

Adoration

◊ ◊ ◊

Now I have come from the Berg String Quartet Opus 3
performed by the Young Artists of the Taos School
home in a sperm of rain
that declares itself to the loaded fireplace
as dead as the world last Friday
though god knows there is a drought in every other state
we live by voices we shall never hear.

May the violent haystack consuming himself as a young man
(that night I went misshapenly to witness the Los Angeles Lakers)
be eaten off the table by the broadening sun
and not the barkeep who bloodies the evening steak.
He was not soundlessly spilling his Miller
onto a manufactured Mexican teen, but I saw and was
hoarse by the time he will reach her alarm

under the stars' neon shoes, stepping lightly over the firmament
of Ogilvie's where the plane trees yellow the margaritas
of the yellow moon behind them, and the brown moon of rain drowns
the elbow moon of that face coming closer to crumbling
before we can choose, before we can announce there is a choice,
before we can prove there is, there was.
I have a handle on my jeans where I would provide

that turn in the town where the tourists meet the art trade
for the firewood they will burn next winter
while skiers fly overhead in an enforced frieze,

a bride a minute beholding Agua Fria Peak in her Angel Fire
t-shirt, while her husband ejaculates from an Air Force jet,
where once there were a few now many,
once a hundred now a state of collapse, a couple of

dogs who pitch and yaw all night for a little water.
For now is the opening the art world belittled, the v-neck and
the bedspread, the stockinged leg, the chain and gear
make-up, the turquoise that lights the lights of the lights
that are lit, our souls nippled with antennae so the world will
hear, the party will know we were the ones who trained like mad to
do it, do it, do it in the perforated gleam of the dollhouse window.

from *Black Warrior Review*

Havana Birth

◊ ◊ ◊

Off Havana the ocean is green this morning
of my birth. The conchers clean their knives on leather
straps and watch the sky while three couples
who have been dancing on the deck of a ship
in the harbor, the old harbor of the fifties, kiss
each other's cheeks and call it a night.

On a green velour sofa five dresses wait
to be fitted. The seamstress kneeling at Mother's feet
has no idea I am about to be born. Mother
pats her stomach which is flat
as the lace mats on the dressmaker's table. She thinks
I'm playing in my room. But as usual, she's wrong.

I'm about to be born in a park in Havana. Oh,
this is important, everything in the dressmaker's house
is furred like a cat. And Havana leans right up
against the windows. In the park, the air
is chocolate, the sweet breath of a man
smoking an expensive cigar. The grass

is drinkable, dazzling, white. In a moment
I'll get up from a bench, lured
by a flock of pigeons, lazily sipping the same syrupy
music through a straw.
Mother is so ignorant, she thinks
I'm rolled like a ball of yarn under the bed. What

does she know of how I got trapped in my life?
She thinks it's all behind her, the bloody
sheets, the mirror in the ceiling
where I opened such a sudden furious blue, her eyes
bruised shut like mine. The pigeon's eyes
are orange, unblinking, a doll's. Mother always said

I wanted to touch everything because
I was a child. But I was younger than that.
I was so young I thought whatever I
wanted, the world wanted too. Workers
in the fields wanted the glint of sun on their machetes.
Sugarcane came naturally sweet, you

had only to lick the earth where it grew.
The music I heard each night outside
my window lived in the mouth of a bird. I was so young
I thought it was easy as walking
into the ocean which always had room
for my body. So when I held out my hands

I expected the pigeon to float between them
like a blossom, dusting my fingers with the manna
of its wings. But the world is wily, and doesn't want
to be held for long, which is why
as my hands reached out, workers lay down
their machetes and left the fields, which is why

a prostitute in a little *calle* of Havana dreamed
the world was a peach and flicked
open a knife. And Mother, startled, shook
out a dress with big pigeons splashed like dirt
across the front, as if she had fallen
chasing after me in the rain. But what could I do?

I was about to be born, I was about to have
my hair combed into the new music
everyone was singing. The dressmaker sang it, her mouth

filled with pins. The butcher sang it and wiped
blood on his apron. Mother sang and thought her body
was leaving her body. And when I tried

I was so young the music beat right
through me, which is how the pigeon got away.
The song the world sings day after day
isn't made of feathers, and the song a bird pours
itself into is tough as a branch
growing with the singer and the singer's delight.

from *Ploughshares*

The Worrying

◇ ◇ ◇

ate me alive day and night these land mines
all over like the toy bombs dropped on the
Afghans little Bozo jack-in-the-boxes
that blow your hands off 3 A.M. I'd go
around the house with a rag of ammonia
wiping wiping crazed as a housewife on *Let's
Make a Deal* the deal being PLEASE DON'T MAKE
HIM SICK AGAIN faucets doorknobs the phone
every lethal thing a person grips and leaves
his prints on scrubbed my hands till my fingers
cracked washed apples ten times ten no salad but
iceberg and shuck the outer two thirds someone
we knew was brain dead from sushi so stick
to meatloaf creamed corn spuds whatever we
could cook to death DO NOT USE THE D WORD
EVEN IN JEST when you started craving deli
I heaved a sigh because salami was so de-
germed with its lovely nitrites to hell with
cholesterol that's for people way way over
the hill or up the hill not us in the vale
of borrowed time yet I was so far more gone
than you nuts in fact ruinous as a supermom
with a kid in a bubble who can't play and ten
years later can't work can't kiss can't laugh
but his room's still clean every cough every
bump would nothing ever be nothing again
cramming you with zinc and Häagen-Dazs so wild

to fatten you up I couldn't keep track of
what was medicine what old wives' but see
THERE WAS NO MEDICINE only me and to
circle the wagons and island the last of our
magic spoon by spoon nap by nap till we
healed you as April heals drinking the sun
I was Prospero of the spell of day-by-day
and all of this just the house worry peanuts
to what's out there and you with the dagger at
your jugular struggling back to work jotting
your calendar two months ahead penciling
clients husbanding husbanding inching back
and me agape with the day's demises who
was swollen who gone mad ringing you on
the hour how are you compared to ten noon
one come home and have blintzes petrified
you'd step in an elevator with some hacking
CPA the whole world ought to be masked
please I can't even speak of the hospital fear
fists bone white the first day of an assault
huddled by your bed like an old crone empty-
eyed in a Greek square black on black the waiting
for tests the chamber of horrors in my head
my rags and vitamins dumb as leeches how did
the meningitis get in where did I slip up
what didn't I scour I'd have swathed the city
in gauze to cushion you no man who hasn't
watched his cruelest worry come true in a room
with no door can ever know what doesn't
die because they lie who say it's over
Rog it hasn't stopped at all are you okay
does it hurt what can I do still still I
think if I worry enough I'll keep you near
the night before Thanksgiving I had this
panic to buy the plot on either side of us
so we won't be cramped that yard of extra grass
would let us breathe THIS IS CRAZY RIGHT but
Thanksgiving morning I went the grave two over

beside you was six feet deep ready for the next
murdered dream so see the threat was real
why not worry worry is like prayer is like
God if you have none they all forget there's
the other side too twelve years and not once
to fret WHO WILL EVER LOVE ME that was
the heaven at the back of time but we had it
here now black on black I wander frantic
never done with worrying but it's mine it's
a cure that's not in the books are you easy
my stolen pal what do you need is it
sleep like sleep you want a pillow a cool
drink oh my one safe place there must be
something just say what it is and it's yours

from *Love Alone*

La Malinche

◊　◊　◊

Money was anything that came to hand

        She had lips for his eyes

(a violent forgetting that forced return)

Because there was no electricity

        A man fucked

Because there was no water

        A woman from behind

The children passed into the train

She was spent

The iron money of the Spartans

We wished we were already there.

        Pressed between them

Black inside the train. The landscape was red. In the dark
sacristy the heavy lace and peculiar smell of holy water.

The green cross of the Inquisition set into the local pink stone.

The circulation of money

The water was infused with a way of life.

Or buried

Yes I know it the Tacuba. Green and black light. Pink and green frosting like stone.

The one you don't want to lose

"Of the Series of Masked Aggressions"

Black tea with heated cream in copper.

Or blending with the street where

The lions. Blue tiles. The House of the Inquisitor has balconies which fly over the street.

As official interpreter she put his orders in the form of rhetorical suggestions tinged with irony.

He put himself inside her mind

Surrounded by souls. A hundred men in black and silver costumes play as they scream.

She had lips painted gold

On the day of the burning everything was draped in green.

Charged with being enlightened.

They close around him

The dark air of the city. She was forbidden to come. There is always a red zone. It means nothing.

Even if "understanding" here means "destroying"

The sound of *geodas*

A white flowered pitcher sells itself. The weaving machine in the hotel Goya. The carriage carries us through the trouble which is black and blue.

Were thighs made unstable

Those who take on the manners of foreigners.

Because beaten or flattered

The Annunciation here retitled Temptation of the Virgin.

He would do.

The twisted train on its back. Corn spills out. A dark woman in her best dress is transparent.

These romantic landscapes also contain elements of desire, skepticism and anguish.

We found them buried in the remains of the river.

They called him by her name.

From inside a shudder

But coins were not the first money.

The monkey put

We meet again for ices. The color is poison.

"Cortez's Henchmen Contemplating the Demons of the New World"

The dead people at the edge of town. The play in the language of the conquerors.

A Saint signed by the Treasurer. Every day there was new money.

Because there was no water

                    She took it

There were no equivalents

The glass coins of Egypt, the knife money of China

                    She had enough

She had lips for his eyes

A man fucked

A woman from behind

Pressed between them

Or buried

The one you don't want to lose

Or blending on the street where

He put himself inside her mind

She had lips painted gold

They close around him

Were thighs made unstable

Because beaten or flattered

From inside a shudder

She took it

She had enough

from *Temblor*

There Will Be Animals

◊ ◊ ◊

There will be animals to teach us
what we can't teach ourselves.

There will be a baboon who is neither stupid nor clumsy
as he paints his mandrill face for the war being waged
against his jungle.

There will be egrets in a few thousand years
who will have evolved without plumes so we cannot take them.

There will be ewes giving and giving their wool
compensating for what we lack in humility.

There will be macaws with short arched bills
that stay short because they talk without telling lies.

Mackerel will continue to appear near Cape Hatteras each spring
and swim north into Canadian waters so there can be continuity.

There will be penguins keeping alive Hollywood's golden era.

The chaparral cock will continue to outdistance man
twisting and turning on a path unconcerned with shortcuts.

Coffin fly dun will leave the Shawsheen River
heading for the lights of Lawrence. What they see in 48 hours
makes them adults who will fast for the rest of their short lives,

mating once during the next hour and understanding everything
as they drop into a communal grave three feet thick with family
reaching the same conclusions.

The coast horned lizard still won't be found
without a bag of tricks; it will inflate and the first
of six million Jewfish will emerge from its mouth.
We will all be richer.

John Dory will replace John Doe
so the nameless among us will have Peter's thumbmark on their
    cheek
and the coin the saint pulled from their mouths in their pockets.
Then once and for all we will know it is no illusion:
the lion lying with the lamb, the grandmother and Little Red
    Riding Hood
walking out of a wolf named Dachau.

from *Pyramid of Bone*

Teratology

◊ ◊ ◊

I

Phineas Gage was a laborer,
the foreman of a road-crew in Vermont.
He was even-tempered and well—

Phineas Gage was a laborer—

Phineas Gage—

Ah, Phineas. I was
a laborer, the foreman
of a road-crew, I was—
I—

Even written down, words
startle up when I
come near them. One word
then. One
word at a time.

Phineas that was I
was about to drop a tamping iron
into the granite hole
of blasting powder
when some odd thing took
our attention

and the other man
forgot to pour the sand to damp the sparks.

Phineas was about to drop the iron—

There. If I could stop it there
by telling it over, if I could stop—

The iron dropped
and struck a spark.

You can see the iron's path:
In here, under the left cheekbone, and out
here, at the top of the skull.

And Phineas—

Where is Phineas?
When the doctor came I said,
"Here's a deal of work for you" and *that*
was Phineas, but not now.

The doctor slid one finger in each end
of the wound's pulpy path and touched
the fingertips inside my brain, inside
the brain of Phineas.

Phineas was a foreman—
The wound closed over but
Phineas was already gone.

One year the lambs had been born
mummified, with no mouths or
eyes, their bones rigid-set so
we had to break them to get them
out of the ewes.
Dozens of them,
like little demons.
A freak accident. An accident

that makes a freak. For a while
I went with the circus and sat
with the tamping iron between my knees
while the barker told the crowds,
"Phinaeas Gage was a foreman
on a road-crew in Vermont . . ."

When I start to laugh I can't
stop.

When I get angry the people
I've known all my life are afraid of me.

Phineas isn't here but I have waited
for him because they say he isn't dead.

But I, I—

Sometimes I think the accident killed me,
but it happened so fast I didn't die.

II

The Wilderness, near Spotsylvania, after nightfall:
The wounded were broadcast through the woods,
raising now and then a cry for help.
But mostly we were quiet.

He walked out of the dark and trees
and when he bent down to look into my face
I asked for water. He said, "It's not you
who's going to drink, my friend."

The incompetent creature didn't drink deeply
enough. Come morning the flesh had shut
over the grapeshot like pond-scum over a dropped stone,
and my one idea was to get out of the light.

They say at one time a squirrel
could have travelled from the Atlantic
to the Mississippi and never touched the ground,
just jumped from tree to tree.

As I could have, had I wished, lived
off the rank fat of the land on one battlefield
after another these hundred years and more.
However, that grew cloying. Even to me.

Oh, I claim no right to comment—except
that of long acquaintance. Next month,
I see, there's to be a conference on Satan
marshalled under the Curial eye

by a public relations firm: "Devils,
Demons, and Dialogues." Dialogues. It seems
the Church would be the Devil's Exegete.
It does not touch on me. Some while back

I taught myself to read, and I've read this:
For a time there were two distinct species of Man,
concurrent; one with huge limbs and a sagittal crest,
but a brain as large as the other, slighter species'.

Both were omnivores, of course. And if they'd both
survived till now, which would be the wolf
I wonder, with a bounty on its hide and its carcasses
strung up on barbed-wire fences through the West;

and which would burn its warm
unflagging lamps under the eaves,
and guard tender grass with pretty
little fences? All its predators are gone.

All but one. Mostly I say nothing
to the kill, but sometimes in an excess
of fury I've said this: "This, my friend,
is what you give the God who has everything."

173

III

At fourteen I stayed awake by brute force
of fascination when Robert Kennedy was shot, and watched
the scene replayed all night; the ashy face
whose disbelieving eyes transfixed the camera
while the stain behind them spread out on the floor.

That was my Medusa, though others would have done
as well: a lolling fly-swarmed skull with open eyes
in Bangladesh, let's say; or the Vietcong prisoner
falling from his knees before his captor's pistol,
the bloody spray held stock-still on film.

Thus from the simple faith of childhood to its naive
and stony unbelief: Underneath everything is not God,
but Horror. And then surcease of that,
by the steady intervention of all that's ordinary.
Under the world's surface lies the world.

Here—and we want to look—is a photograph
of a Haitian soldier, standing over those citizens
who'd come to vote the day before. Beside one ruined face
a red mass congeals, which the magazine declines
to caption. It is the world, and we are in it.

from *Fine Madness*

They

◊ ◊ ◊

They've put their songbird next to the window
In its cage, and the green square of the park
Is full of children, I could say *also,*
Or simply, *as though it too . . . ,*
Either way I'd have out my black dress,
Wouldn't I? A bravely widowed bit of fine lace
Firmly pressed to my eyes. Don't worry
About the phone call you missed—she said
You were out walking—I might try again, later,
Or not, you understand. It was only an impulse,
Caught, like the one just now at the screen
Door—I was gazing out through the fine mesh
At the park and the children and changing
My mind,—my hand (and there's an adverb here,
But what? *lightly, hesitantly, nervously?*)
Toying with the knob. I wanted to talk to you
About style, and what my insistence on beauty
And pathos won't let me say, or just hear
Your voice, even. But see how little of the song-
Bird or the children I've given you so far?
The bird has a single brief note it repeats
Rapidly, frantically (no, that's my word for me
Hearing it), fixed by odd silences,
And which ends plaintively (no, that's me again:
I end plaintively) on something between
A squeak and a whine. I know its name,
And the names of a lot of the birds in the sky

And the trees and so there are ways
I am permitted to use them, but I don't know whose
Children those are in the park, and I really want
Only to know when they will go home, so I
Can go out and not have to feel
They are "they" or I am one of them, either side
Of the line I am, actually. That's what I want. And
That you might call me back or that it might start
Raining, these chances just decorate the surface
Of my longing but are, I keep reminding myself,
Its meaning anyhow, its limits, its style.
The cage is tiny but the bird is so small
I can barely see it: but for the sudden lurch
And the tilted sway of its little trapeze
(And the noise, of course, of course) I couldn't
Insist it was really there. *Under the low clouds*
They were lit in the last of the sunlight a soft gold—
So I prove my desire to see them. In the frame
Of the swingset, one, kicking hard, flung himself
Back and forth: grey sky, the vividly green lawn,
And grey sky. I was pressing my face to the metal
Screen of the screendoor (these plaintive noises
All about me pressing my face to the screen),
And nothing was changed or lost but everything was
Little pictures exactly the same size.

from *The Threepenny Review*

(2 pages from a long poem in progress)

◊ ◊ ◊

"A mother"   "& child"   "were both on fire, continuously"
"The fire   "was contained in them"   "sealed them off
from others"   "But you could see the flame"   "halo
of short flames all about the"   "conjoined bodies, who

sat" "they sat apart" "on a seat for two" "at end of car" "The
ghost"   "of the father"   "sat in flames"   "beside them"
"paler flames"   "sat straight ahead"   "looking
straight ahead, not"   "moving."   "A woman"

"another woman"   "in a uniform from"   "above the ground"
"entered" "the train" "She was fireproof" "She was gloves, & she"
"took"   "the baby"   "took the baby"   "away from the"
"Mother" "Extracted" "the burning baby" "from the fire" "they

made together"   "But the baby"   "still burned"
("But not yours"   "It didn't happen"   "to you")
"We don't know yet"   "if it will"   "stop burning"
"said the uniformed""woman""The burning woman""was crying"

"she made a form" "in her mind" "an imaginary" "form" "to
settle"   "in her arms where"   "the baby"   "had been"   "We saw
her fiery arms"   "cradle air"   "She cradled air"   ("They take your
children"   "away"   "if you're on fire")

177

"In the air that"   "she cradled"   "it seemed to us there"   "floated"
"a flower-like"   "a red flower"   "its petals"   "curling flames"
"She cradled" "seemed to cradle" "the burning flower of" "herself
     gone"
"her life"   ("She saw"   "whatever she saw, but what we saw"
     "was that flower")

★   ★   ★

"A woman came into"   "the car"   "about thirty-seven"   "maybe
forty" "Face" "a harsh response to" "what she did" "had to do"
"face rigid,"   "but she was beautiful" "Was," "we could see,"
"one of the ones who"   "strip for coins"   "on the subway" —

"They simply"   "very quickly"   ("illegally")   "remove all their
clothes" "Stand, for a moment" "Turning to face" "each end"
"of the car"   "Then dress quickly,"   "pass quickly"   "the cup."
"But she—this one—"   "face of hating to so much that"   "as she

took off her blouse,"   "her face"   "began to change"   "Grew
feathers, a small beak" "& by the time she was naked," "she wore the
head" "of an eagle" "a crowned eagle" "a raptor" "herself" —
"And as she stood" "& faced the car" "her body" "was changing"

"was becoming entirely" "that bird" "those wings," "she shrank to
become the bird"   "but grew wings that"   "were wider"   "than
     she had been"
"tall" "Instantly," "instantly, a man caught her" "A cop came"
"As if ready"   "as if they knew"   "Her wings were clipped,"

"talons cut"   "as if as quickly"   "as possible"   "She was released
then, to the car"   "to the subway"   "Perched"   "on the bar the
straps hang from"

from *How(ever)*

Six Hermetic Songs

◇ ◇ ◇

for Robert Duncan

Bring along the Makhent boat
for I have come to see Osiris
lord of the *ansi* garment

How did we measure
It says we measured up and down
from the sepia disk
to the crowded ship
of Odysseus

How did we measure
It says we measured
with a copper thread
from the plum flower
to the forgotten gift

Was the tain's smoke
equal to song
the vein of cedar
to a pin's bones
Burns each

earlier day
in its soundless weight
measured by the nets
of air
Go there

You can bring down a house with a sound.
Not to understand this.
But we builded it.

Not with periods (the
sentence) or any sense of design—
sight or sound.

Builded it while blind.
Rain came in.
Noises not ours.

Steps called walls.
Model of a house.
Work we had done before.

In—
harmonics as when
as children

still writing,
writed, written,
interrupted, begun.

The body in fog and the tongue
bracketed in its form

The words as if silvered—coated
and swallowed, cradled and erased

The marks whereby the body
was said to be a world

The walled rehearsals
The curve of abandon,

twinned and masked
The calls and careless fashionings,

digits thrown like dice
I don't think about that anymore

Send me my dictionary
Write how you are

There were nine grand pianos in my father's house
one a water object in my head
and one a ship of glass

one an eye on the end of a branch
and one a paint pot spilling red
There were live fandangos in the father's house

so that sleepers might sleep within the dance
and set their images to rest
Please tell me if you can

Did it snow pure snow in some father's house
and did the children chant Whether me this
then Whether me that

There was a winding stair in this father's house
climbing or falling no one would say
There were notebooks and nightbooks

and voices enclosed by a ring of bone
They were crying Wait Don't Wait
There were travelers standing at the gate.

At the fever of tongues
the metron, with wandering eye

————————

At the zero of streets and of windows
an arm in geometry

————————

At the circus of nets
at the torn first
edge of an image
the unit of distance
between the eye and the lid

————————

At the swarm of the messengers

————————

At the storm of fine dust

————————

At the pillars and the receiving paths

————————

At the hidden roads of the disk

————————

At the body of the speaking boat

The wrecked horn of the body
and a water voice

The horn of the body
and a slanted water voice

The notes against the gate
and the erasures at the gate

Mineral swimmers fixed
in a stone's milk

and the doorways of our disappearing
Whose night-songs and bridges

and prisms are these
Whose evens and odds

cats on high limbs
scorpions and swallows

What figures within the coil
tortoise and Bennu bird

lotus and hawk
palette plus ink-pot

from *Sulfur*

Pilgrimage

◊ ◊ ◊

Near the peak. A clear morning,
Camphorous air of eucalyptus and mountain laurel
Lining the steep trail.

They chant in chorus as they climb,
Some of them in turns bearing
The ark—its hammered silver
Ornaments jangling, the pressure
Of polished cedar beams heavily
Afloat on their shoulders,
The others reaching in
To touch it as they dance and kiss
Their fingers that brushed it.

At the last of the dusty switchbacks
The trail grows wider and flatter
And they pause, flushed and shuffling.
They lower the ark to the earth,
A priest singing his aria
From beside it: Now I call you by your
True name—and they come forward:

One by one he fits
Embroidered blinders over their eyes
And guiding them singly by the hand
Singing the secret name of each
He leads them from the ark upward

To the cliff's edge, till the whole choir
Stands dancing in place
At the precipice, each man and woman
Chanting in a darkness.

At the prayer's end
They lift the blinders
To see the falls across the sheer vacancy:

Mountain light, the bridal veil
Skimming the great vertical
Rockface without interval,
Unquenchable granite in its plumage
Of air and falling water:
                                O Presence
You have searched me and seen me from afar,
My downsitting and my uprising.
Now nothing is next or before, there is
Nothing yet to enter, you have beset me
Behind and before, you have put
Your hand upon me, though I am
Fearfully and wonderfully made,
You have known me from afar.

Now for many of them
The falls appear motionless: hung
From the foamless brim in a vision
Of suspended flowing, falling
But unfallen. Through tears
Of pleasure they squint upward.

Now when they take the thick wizened scroll
Out from the ark in its white armor
And unfurl it, the crowned letters
Scorched and stained into the skin
In a catalogue of secret names—
                                Akhman, Ruveyne,

Yeosif, each sound indicated by characters
That form another sound, never to be uttered,
And behind each unutterable name
The name of that name's
Name in infinite regress—

They read themselves into the unchangeable
Book of the journey begun before
Your body was called up
And before it was made,
Before you were a seed packed in honey, before you

Fell from the brim, fashioned and torn
From the cold water that tumbles
Endlessly down the face of the mountain.

from *Antæus*

Service Includes Free Lifetime Updating

◇   ◇   ◇

Erase the lines under your titles. That's right.
The books are the next to go.
Erase chapter headings, Roman numerals, index
cards, business letters. Down the telephone cords.

Continents are breaking up everywhere. In Arizona towns
the dinosaurs are smoking cigarettes
at the counters of small penny stores.
They look at their reflections and do not laugh.

On a column above the Botanical Gardens
in Brooklyn, a serious statue
reads a magazine. "The best way
is robed in black." The print sings.

Santa Claus is interviewed in medical journals.
He tells parents to keep lying. His suit is white
but his shoes are black. All the psychologists agree.
It is easier to have surgery than to change your mind,

the young women say to their special cigarettes.
The wind whips the sticks of their thin black-stocking legs
in their pointed boots. The leaves fall undecided.
A Greek statue in the urinal loses one marble arm.

The tin hosts march up the hill
eating pea soup. Since they do not rust
they are interpreted as a dream.
Even this does not provoke them to use their bayonets.

In Texas, a man,
nobody's grandfather
in particular, mouths the creed: The righteous shall come to no harm.
The congregation shines its chromium swords

to slice the unresisting bread
and drink the pitying wine
with their shined lips.
His quiet is misinterpreted

again and again. In Cambridge
a team of scientists is earnestly eliciting life from
clay. The computer-generated Darwinian weed
undergoes evolution quietly. Nobody notices.

Two mammoth memorial statues
are tired of victory. They descend,
impersonal, sexless, from their marble billboard.
Elsewhere, the words

are running off cue cards.
People try to catch them. The director
shouts through the telephone. Down the long cords
of his neck. Objects are solid. Details at elven

(a deliberate mistake)
we can't control our hands any more.
No more plurals. One of Ayn Rand's minor characters
wakes up and finds herself in a bad play

at Camp Appaloosa. You have used the beginning of my life,
she tells them, and rewritten the ending
as a dream. My mind does not change.
She opens her mouth but no sound comes out.

The legions of dreams discover us. Where are the lesions
of our mountain-climb? Did we climb over
the pointed top or around the low stone? We are at the base.
They are discovering us. We cannot expect them to weep.

from *Hanging Loose*

JAPANESE PRESENTATION,
I & II

◊   ◊   ◊

Izubuchi says Pound's poems

are inadvertent Rengas

goat-foot   choros   the

not a ray
not a
spare disc
pale foot
this is the first time

(direct quotation of   passage)

when the fisherman hesitates

he might

be deceived
doubt is immortal
                              compared with
        sunlight
not complete sense
no deceit in heaven
which enables the wearer
point of contact
act of forgiveness

again
after
an attempt
consolation
divine comedy
neither feather nor flame
which is actually
a holy mountain in Buddhism
tree connects heaven & earth
oak   olive   katura

(to summarize Pound's whole

life)

inspiteof
hear the wind speak
a pretty look in her eyes
at the mercy of the wind blow

ing

post-humous

pine   spruce
eternal voice
a corona of angels
a drama in which:

/he/	suddenly recalled Buddhist rule	/to/
	abstain from drinking	
/he/	declines the drink from	/the/
	wedding cup	
/to/	join the two traditions	/to/get/her

Dante met Beatrice
(bitter memory discarded)
though his body remained on the earth
& wept in the rain

from *O.blek*

The Old Causes

◊　◊　◊

My soul is wearied because of murderers.
JEREMIAH 4:31

In the cool future, one will put off her dress by a window
and another will make the choice
between inhabiting and admiring.

We don't live long enough, any of us, to outlast history.
We shall not love with our bodies again
except in the coronal streets of paintings,

the unjust happiness and lamplight of the ratty voyeur
for ones so terribly thin now
without the little flags of their clothes.

Great tyrants understood the flesh and our nostalgia for it.
The glory of the rainy square
alive with atoms of loud speech
The glory of oblique pillars
of sunlight on the tousled hairs of a bed
The glory of not taking you in my arms now
but letting the paradise of the next day
waken to find you already there
teaching me to live with no purpose
and the endless rain on the public square better than heaven.

I dream of the deprived utopias that may yet arrive.
I see myself repeating a kind of courtship.
There is a messy apartment
brightened here and there by the subjective icons
of a woman's life before I knew her.
Somehow, I translate all of that
into the struggle and final triumph
of all of the people shouting one name,
not my name, but one I know intimately,
and then it is my right to go to bed with her.

In the cool future, the apartments and unfeeling icons
will face each other across our bodies.
We shall count for very little

or maybe I shall have learned to make the right choice, tendering
the little flags of her clothes
between my hands like a birthplace

or like the silhouette of my mother by the broken glass
of the apartment she died in
crowned with the future's coronal of lamplight.

from *Boulevard*

Living Memory

◇ ◇ ◇

Open the book of tales you knew by heart,
begin driving the old roads again,
repeating the old sentences, which have changed
minutely from the wordings you remembered.
A full moon on the first of May
drags silver film on the Winooski River.
The villages are shut
for the night, the woods are open
and soon you arrive at a crossroads
where late, late in time you recognize
part of yourself is buried. Call in Danville,
village of water-witches.

From here on instinct is uncompromised and clear:
the tales come crowding like the Kalevala
longing to burst from the tongue. Under the trees
of the backroad you rumor the dark
with houses, sheds, the long barn
moored like a barge on the hillside.
Chapter and verse. A mailbox. A dooryard.
A drink of springwater from the kitchen tap.
An old bed, old wallpaper. Falling asleep like a child
in the heart of the story.

Reopen the book. A light mist soaks the page,
blunt naked buds tip the wild lilac scribbled
at the margin of the road, no one knows when.

Broken stones of drywall mark the onset
of familiar paragraphs slanting up and away
each with its own version, nothing ever
has looked the same from anywhere.

We came like others to a country of farmers—
Puritans, Catholics, Scotch, Irish, Québecois:
bought a failed Yankee's empty house and barn
from a prospering Yankee,
Jews following Yankee footprints,
prey to many myths but most of all
that Nature makes us free. That the land can save us.
Pioneer, indigenous; we were neither.

You whose stories these farms secrete,
you whose absence these fields publish,
all you whose lifelong travail
took as given this place and weather
who did what you could with the means you had—
it was pick and shovel work
done with a pair of horses, a stone boat
a strong back, and an iron bar: clearing pasture—
Your memories crouched, foreshortened in our text.
Pages torn. New words crowding the old.

I knew a woman whose clavicle was smashed
inside a white clapboard house with an apple tree
and a row of tulips by the door. I had a friend
with six children and a tumor like a seventh
who drove me to my driver's test and in exchange
wanted to see Goddard College, in Plainfield. She'd heard
women without diplomas could study there.
I knew a woman who walked
straight across cut stubble in her bare feet away,
women who said, *He's a good man, never*
laid a hand to me as living proof.
A man they said fought death
to keep fire for his wife for one more winter, leave
a woodpile to outlast him.

I was left the legacy of a pile of stovewood
split by a man in the mute chains of rage.
The land he loved as landscape
could not unchain him. There are many,
Gentile and Jew, it has not saved. Many hearts have burst
over these rocks, in the shacks
on the failure sides of these hills. Many guns
turned on brains already splitting
in silence. Where are those versions?
Written-across like nineteenth-century letters
or secrets penned in vinegar, invisible
till the page is held over flame.

I was left the legacy of three sons
—as if in an old legend of three brothers
where one changes into a rufous hawk
one into a snowy owl
one into a whistling swan
and each flies to the mother's side
as she travels, bringing something she has lost,
and she sees their eyes are the eyes of her children
and speaks their names and they become her sons.
But there is no one legend and one legend only.

This month the land still leafless, out from snow
opens in all directions, the transparent woods
with sugar-house, pool, cellar-hole unscreened.
Winter and summer cover the closed roads
but for a few weeks they lie exposed,
the old nervous-system of the land. It's the time
when history speaks in a row of crazy fence-poles
a blackened chimney, houseless, a spring
soon to be choked in second growth
a stack of rusting buckets, a rotting sledge.

It's the time when your own living
laid open between seasons
ponders clues like the *One Way* sign defaced
to *Bone Way,* the stones

of a graveyard in Vermont, a Jewish cemetery
in Birmingham, Alabama.
How you have needed these places,
as a tall gaunt woman used to need to sit
at the knees of bronze-hooded *Grief*
by Clover Adams' grave.
But you will end somewhere else, a sift of ashes
awkwardly flung by hands you have held and loved
or, nothing so individual, bones reduced
with, among, other bones, anonymous,
or wherever the Jewish dead
have to be sought in the wild grass overwhelming
the cracked stones. Hebrew spelled in wilderness.

All we can read is life. Death is invisible.
A yahrzeit candle belongs
to life. The sugar skulls
eaten on graves for the Day of the Dead
belong to life. To the living. The Kaddish is to the living,
the Day of the Dead, for the living. Only the living
invent these plumes, tombs, mounds, funeral ships,
living hands turn the mirrors to the walls,
tear the boughs of yew to lay on the casket,
rip the clothes of mourning. Only the living
decide death's color: is it white or black?
The granite bulkhead
incised with names, the quilt of names, were made
by the living, for the living.
                              I have watched
films from a Pathé camera, a picnic
in sepia, I have seen my mother
tossing an acorn into the air;
my grandfather, alone in the heart of his family;
my father, young, dark, theatrical;
myself, a six-month child.
Watching the dead we see them living
their moments, they were at play, nobody thought
they would be watched so.
                              When Selma threw

her husband's ashes into the Hudson
and they blew back on her and on us, her friends,
it was life. Our blood raced in that gritty wind.

Such details get bunched, packed, stored
in these cellar-holes of memory
so little is needed
to call on the power, though you can't name its name:
It has its ways of coming back:
a truck going into gear on the crown of the road
the white-throat sparrow's notes
the moon in her fullness standing
right over the concrete steps the way
she stood the night they landed there.
                                        From here
nothing has changed, and everything.

The scratched and treasured photograph Richard showed me
taken in '29, the year I was born:
it's the same road I saw
strewn with the Perseids one August night,
looking older, steeper than now
and rougher, yet I knew it. Time's
power, the only just power—would you
give it away?

from *American Poetry Review*

199

Switchblade

◇ ◇ ◇

Most of the past is lost,
and I'm glad mine has vanished
into blackness or space or whatever nowhere
what we feel and do goes,
but there were a few cool Sunday afternoons
when my father wasn't sick with hangover
and the air in the house wasn't foul with anger
and the best china had been cleared after the week's best meal
so he could place on the table his violins
to polish with their special cloth and oil.
Three violins he'd arrange
side by side in their velvet-lined cases
with enough room between for the lids to lie open.
They looked like children in coffins,
three infant sisters whose hearts had stopped for no reason,
but after he rubbed up their scrolls and waists
along the lines of the grain to the highest sheen,
they took on the knowing posture of women in silk gowns
in magazine ads for new cars and ocean voyages,
and, as if a violin were a car in storage
that needed a spin around the block every so often,
for fifteen minutes he would play each one—
though not until each horsehair bow was precisely tightened
and coated with rosin, and we had undergone an eon of tuning.
When he played no one was allowed to speak to him.
He seemed to see something drastic across the room
or feel it through his handkerchief padding the chinboard.

So we'd hop in front of him waving or making pig-noses
the way kids do to guards at Buckingham Palace,
and after he had finished playing and had returned to himself,
he'd softly curse the idiocy of his children
beneath my mother's voice yelling to him from the kitchen
That was beautiful, Paul, play it again.

He never did, and I always hoped he wouldn't,
because the whole time I was waiting for his switchblade
to appear, and the new stories he'd tell me
for the scar thin as a seam
up the white underside of his forearm,
for the chunks of proud flesh on his back and belly,
scarlet souvenirs of East St. Louis dance halls in the twenties,
cornered in men's rooms, ganged in blind alleys,
always slashing out alone with this knife.
First the violins had to be snug again
inside their black cases
for who knew how many more months or years or lifetimes;
then he had to pretend to have forgotten
why I was sitting there wide-eyed across from him
long after my sister and brother had gone off with friends.
Every time, as if only an afterthought,
he'd sneak into his pocket and ease the switchblade
onto the bare table between us,
its thumb-button jutting from the pearl-and-silver plating
like the eye of some sleek prehistoric fish.
I must have known it wouldn't come to life
and slither toward me by itself,
but when he'd finally nod to me to take it
its touch was still warm with his body heat
and I could feel the blade inside aching
to flash open with the terrible click
that sounds now like just a *tsk* of disappointment,
it has become so sweet and quiet.

from *God Hunger*

Last Night with Rafaella

◊ ◊ ◊

Last night, with Rafaella,

I sat at one of the outside tables
At *Rosati* watching the *ragazzi* on Vespas
Scream through the Piazza del Popolo

And talked again about changing my life,

Doing something meaningful—perhaps
Exploring a continent or discovering a vaccine,
Falling in love or over the white falls
Of a dramatic South American river!—
And Rafaella

Stroked the back of my wrist as I talked,

Smoothing the hairs until they lay as quietly
As wheat before the old authoritarian wind.

Rafaella had just returned from Milano
Where she'd supervised the Spring collection
Of a famous, even notorious, young designer—

A man whose name brought tears to the eyes
Of Contessas, movie stars, and diplomats' wives
Along the Via Condotti or the Rue
Du Faubourg-St. Honoré.

So I felt comfortable there, with Rafaella,
Discussing these many important things, I mean
The spiritual life, and my own
Long disenchantment with the ordinary world.

Comfortable because I knew she was a sophisticated,
Well-travelled woman, so impossible
To shock. A friend who'd
Often rub the opal on her finger so slowly

It made your mouth water,

The whole while telling you what it would be like
To feel her tongue addressing your ear.

And how could I not trust the advice
Of a woman who, with the ball of her exquisite thumb,
Carefully flared rouge along the white cheekbones
Of the most beautiful women in the world?

Last night, as we lay in the dark,
The windows of her bedroom open to the cypress,
To the stars, to the wind knocking at those stiff
Umbrella pines along her garden's edge,
I noticed as she turned slowly in the moonlight

A small tattoo just above her hip bone—

It was a dove in flight or an angel with its
Head tucked beneath its wing,

I couldn't tell in the shadows . . .

And as I kissed this new illumination of her body
Rafaella said, *Do you know how to tell a model?*
In fashion, they wear tattoos like singular beads
Along their hips,
                    but artists' models

Wear them like badges against the daily nakedness,
The way Celestine has above one nipple that
Minute yellow bee and above
The other an elaborate, cupped poppy . . .

I thought about this,
Pouring myself a little wine and listening
To the owls marking the distances, the geometries
Of the dark.
                              Rafaella's skin was
Slightly damp as I ran my fingertip
Along each delicate winged ridge of her
Collarbone, running the harp length of ribs
Before circling the shy angel . . .

And slowly, as the stars
Shifted in their rack of black complexities above,

Along my shoulder, Rafaella's hair fell in coils,

Like the frayed silk of some ancient tapestry,
Like the spun cocoons of the Orient—
Like a fragile ladder

To some whole other level of the breath.

from *The Gettysburg Review*

Haze

◇ ◇ ◇

hangs heavy
down into trees: dawn
doesn't break today,
the morning
seeps into being, one
bird, maybe
two, chipping
away at it. A white dahlia,
big
as Baby Bumstead's head,
leans
its folded petals
at a window, a lesson
in origami.
Frantically, God
knows what
machine: oh no,
just Maggio's
garbage truck.
Stare
at all the roughage
that hides an estuary,
and such urbanity
seems inapt: the endless city
builds on and on,
thinning out, here and there,
for the wet green velvet towels

("slight imperfections")
of summer
("moderately priced")
and a hazy morning
in August,
even that
we may grow to love.

from *The New Yorker*

AIDS Days

◇ ◇ ◇

I

"Perfection Eludes Us"

The most beautiful power in the world has buttocks.
It is always a dream come true.
They are big. They are too big.
Kiss them and spank them till they are scalding.
Till she can't breathe saying oh.
Till your hand is in love.
Till your eyes are raw.
Stockings and garter belt without underpants are
The secret ceremony but who would imagine
She is wearing a business suit. She is in her office. She merely
    touches
The high-tech phone. Without a word,
She lies down across the hassock and eases her skirt up.
How big it is.
Her eyes are closed. . . . She has the votes.
They know she does. They're waiting for her now next door.
The number is ringing.
She squeezes them together. She squeezes them together.
She presses herself against the hassock.
She starts to spank herself.

II

The American Sonnet

She has the votes; they know she does;
They're waiting for her now next door.
Her eyes are closed.
We were discussing the arms race when the moderator died,
Presumably a performance piece, was
What it's called. He said it is.
It actually wasn't so political was only
Broadcast without a live audience.
The telephone is warbling.
The secretary has allowed the call through which means
      the President.
Herself is on the line.
Her dreams are calling her. The press will be there.
Her skirt is all the way up.
I am the epopt. Thou art the secret ceremony.

III

Aleph, Beth, Gimel, Daleth . . .

A man sits memorizing a naked woman—
A slot cut in a wall
Which has a metal slide which opens
When he puts a quarter in
Lets him look for hours.
It seems like hours.
He keeps forgetting what he sees.
He pays and stares
Into the brightly lit beyond
Dancing on a stage just beyond the wall, bare feet
On a level with his chin.
He looks up at it,
Without the benefit of music

Just standing there.
And then the music starts again.
The wall in which the slot is cut is curved.
So when the slot is open, besides a dance he sees
Curving away from him to either side an ocean liner row
Of little windows.
Prisoners in solitary confinement
Might get their meals through one of these—
Presumably behind each one a booth like his.
The open slots are dark.
A slot of darkness in the wall
Is someone.
Someone hidden is hunching there.
From some slots money waves.
The woman ripples over and squats
In front of it, her knees spread wide.
She takes the bill—
Sometimes she presses herself against the slot.
A man stays in a booth.
The door stays locked. The slot stays open.
He can't remember what he memorized.
It seems like hours.
It is too late.

IV

L'Hallali

Serve me the ice cream bitterer than vinegar
Beneath a royal palm covered with needles.
Tell me a love story that ends with acyclovir
Five times a day for five days.

You never had it so good.
He made me my dog which He took.
Houseflies and herpes He brings.
Buttery ice cream smooth as Vaseline.

Florida. Dawn. Five hundred clouds.
Anal chocolate turning pink.
Oxygen-rich, from an opened artery
In the warm water

In the claw-footed tub. Dawn
Spreads from Gorbachev these arms talks AIDS days.
Will it spread?
Venus on the half-shell, moist and pink rose of salt—

Belons 000 when they're freshest are as sweet.
Chincoteagues from the bay are as plump.
Freshly squeezed is as sweet.
This is your life. You live in France,

Klaus Barbie, in 1983, and '84, and '85, and '86, and '87.
And every day is the bissextus.
And every dawn is Hiroshima.
Hallali!

from *These Days*

The Initiate

◇ ◇ ◇

St. John of the Cross wore dark glasses
As he passed me on the street.
St. Theresa of Avila, beautiful and grave,
Turned her back on me.

"Soulmate," they hissed. "It's high time."

I was a blind child, a wind-up toy . . .
I was one of death's juggling red balls
On a certain street corner
Where they peddle things out of suitcases.

The city like a huge cinema
With lights dimmed.
The performance already started.

So many blurred faces in a complicated plot.

The great secret which kept eluding me: knowing who I am . . .

The Redeemer and the Virgin,
Their eyes wide open in the empty church
Where the killer came to hide himself . . .

The new snow on the sidewalk bore footprints
That could have been made by bare feet.
Some unknown penitent guiding me.

In truth, I didn't know where I was going.
My feet were frozen,
My stomach growled.

Four young hoods blocking my way.
Three deadpan, one smiling crazily.

I let them have my black raincoat.

Thinking constantly of the Divine Love and the Absolute had
      disfigured me.
People mistook me for someone else.
I heard voices after me calling out unknown names.
"I'm searching for someone to sell my soul to,"
The drunk who followed me whispered,
While appraising me from head to foot.

At the address I had been given.
The building had large X's over its windows.
I knocked but no one came to open.
By and by a black girl joined me on the steps.
She banged at the door till her fist hurt.

Her name was Alma, a propitious sign.
She knew someone who solved life's riddles
In a voice of an ancient Sumerian queen.
We had a long talk about that
While shivering and stamping our wet feet.

It was necessary to stay calm, I explained,
Even with the earth trembling,
And to continue to watch oneself
As if one were a complete stranger.

Once in Chicago, for instance,
I caught sight of a man in a shaving mirror
Who had my naked shoulders and face,
But whose eyes terrified me!

Two hard staring, all-knowing eyes!

After we parted, the night, the cold, and the endless walking
Brought on a kind of ecstasy.
I went as if pursued, trying to warm myself.

There was the East River; there was the Hudson.
Their waters shone like oil in sanctuary lamps.

Something supreme was occurring
For which there will never be any words.

The sky was full of racing clouds and tall buildings,
Whirling and whirling silently.

In that whole city you could hear a pin drop.
Believe me,
I thought I heard a pin drop and I went looking for it.

from *Antæus*

GUSTAF SOBIN

Transparent Itineraries: 1984

◊   ◊   ◊

for Claude Royet-Journoud

grammar itself at
the very tip of   each card, the
    months rushed, slipped
under. . . . according to the predicate, would
grapple or   stray, sip sometimes   at one another's
                                                    reflections.

---

as if to match image with its ever-dissolving models.

(what fell, weightlessly as waves, through its own fires . . .).

as arbitrary, as determinant.

whole weeks spent—suspended—between one chord and the next
(Gesualdo).

took 'wind' out, took 'clouds.' left 'this' (was where we'd
sleep).

---

a face, so sudden, moving
against no   panel, accumulating
                                        no   appreciable depth.

---

or a wrist, twisting—in half-turns—through jade.

each feature, teased to a focus.

(breeze-needles).

as if what we'd fashioned, utterly infused, might—of it-
self—emit, radiate, *inform*.

---

tensest of
petals,
tasted one
an-

other in the
deep

crease of
those
screens. . . .

---

breath-struck, the arms, shoulders, sex: the guesses we'd
made, the definitions we'd given ourselves.

draft-star, our speculated drift. . . .

would change stations, octaves, the whole scale of that son-
orous ocean.

(were the lightmen, you wrote, who'd arrived first).

"*tout était faux, absurde, épatant, délicieux,*" Matisse.

skidding tips of the breakers, those gates, entries, those
long rooms we'd driven towards, all night. . . .

(piled hearts, that heaped linen).

where the gray eyes, gone under, emptied their image.

'like foam,' or later: 'like lost footage.'

no longer needed us, our spent pronouns, for pulling its
moons through.

---

so much light, gone
un–
gathered: words
no one
would wear. . . .

---

where some sound (some labial) might have kept the cave open.

those blown, ochre-speckled planetaria.

(thin slips of the parallel).

as, through the otherwise unoscillating wastes, would quaver.

carried that image, that other, that crumpled gold like some
pressed tissue, meticulously tooled.

(some tiny, mummified gland).

'like fire, falling.'

where, to a low row of stars, the eyes shrank.

from *Voyaging Portraits*

Primos

◇ ◇ ◇

off Land's End

As an unlucky match is singled out and struck
against a matchbox, we struck the Seven Stones
on the 24th of June, in the Year of our Lord, 1871,
and quickly foundered, the crew of eleven drowned,
except for you, Vincenzo Defilice, the odd man
who left all behind to swim away and toward
nothing, no one, hope your only handhold
against the sliding, slippery waves of a chance throw.
An unreal parade of cargo floated past,
laughably useless, a chair and writing table,
corked bottle of spirits, a bobbing pair of boots
a ghost might use to lightly walk across the water.
Why, why were you not yet drowned, too?
Numbly, you sifted the acts of a lifetime,
the pettiness and petty generosities, anger, greed,
and self-defeating loves, searching for a sign or clue
your life was worse or better than the next man's.
And then a miracle began to happen: a human form,
no mermaid, appearing beside you in the waves,
wearing a gilded crown, her face uplifted
to the clouds, serene as a saint's. Wake up, Vincenzo!
Again I am pulled backward through time's current
to buoy your artless, dreaming heart.
Face to face, we lock in an embrace more urgent
and prolonged than any two landlocked lovers

ever exchanged, riding the swells for hours,
then parting, exhausted, your reasons expedient:
you swam toward land or land's illusion,
a rich man in possession of a story more fabulous
than the disenchanted fictions of any shipwrecked novelist.
Years pass as quickly as the turning of pages.
Now in the underwater dark of taverns and bars,
you cross yourself and tell your tale of water
to sure-footed unbelievers hungry to hear
a drunken sailor's story of wholly improbable rescue.
The world is full of grace and second chances
for a few. You were a saved man.
I speculate upon your future.

from *American Poetry Review*

Saving My Skin from Burning

◇ ◇ ◇

There was a hole in the ground once; there was a manhole
I used to get inside. I lowered a rope
and kicked my way down. The walls were two feet thick
and there was at most a foot of leaves where somehow
the wind had crept in, but there was no water. I felt for
the pipe, there was a little ledge—with matches.
I tried to get out. The truth was I fell. My mind
was on vipers, I called my enemies vipers, it was
an old honorific word but now I shook,
they were not just snakes—they were adders—their bodies
were flat, their fangs were huge, my enemies
strike like they do—their heads are triangles,
their eyes are in their skulls. I screamed for rope,
I needed rags, I had to save my skin
from burning—my chest and upper arms.
                                        The hole
is our greatest fear; I grab the air behind me
and stiffen my legs. The greatest joy is rising,
the greatest joy is resting your arms on the ground
and getting ready to swing your body up
and seeing the clouds again and feeling the wind
on your white legs, and rubbing your eyes. I ran
to touch a tree, I stroked the bark, there was
one stone, it was half-pitted, the sun had turned it
into a pillow; I lay on my back recovering.

from *The Iowa Review*

Orpheus Alone

◊ ◊ ◊

It was an adventure much could be made of: a walk
On the shores of the darkest known river,
Among the hooded, shoving crowds, by steaming rocks
And rows of ruined huts half buried in the muck;
Then to the great court with its marble yard
Whose emptiness gave him the creeps, and to sit there
In the sunken silence of the place and speak
Of what he had lost, what he still possessed of his loss,
And then, pulling out all the stops, describing her eyes,
Her forehead, where the golden light of evening spread,
The curve of her neck, the slope of her shoulders, everything
Down to her thighs and calves, letting the words come,
As if lifted from sleep, to drift upstream,
Against the water's will, where all the condemned
And pointless labor, stunned by his voice's cadence,
Would come to a halt, and even the crazed, dishevelled
Furies, for the first time, would weep, and the soot-filled
Air would clear just enough for her, the lost bride,
To step through the image of herself and be seen in the light.
As everyone knows, this was the first great poem,
Which was followed by days of sitting around
In the houses of friends, with his head back, his eyes
Closed, trying to will her return, but finding
Only himself, again and again, trapped
In the chill of his loss, and, finally,
Without a word, taking off to wander the hills
Outside of town, where he stayed until he had shaken

The image of love and put in its place the world
As he wished it would be, urging its shape and measure
Into speech of such newness that the world was swayed,
And trees suddenly appeared in the bare place
Where he spoke and lifted their limbs and swept
The tender grass with the gowns of their shade,
And stones, weightless for once, came and set themselves there,
And small animals lay in the miraculous fields of grain
And aisles of corn, and slept. The voice of light
Had come forth from the body of fire, and each thing
Rose from its depths and shone as it never had.
And that was the second great poem,
Which no one recalls anymore. The third and greatest
Came into the world as the world, out of the unsayable,
Invisible source of all longing to be, it came
As things come that will perish, to be seen or heard
Awhile, like the coating of frost or the movement
Of wind, and then no more; it came in the middle of sleep
Like a door to the infinite, and, circled by flame,
Came again at the moment of waking, and sometimes,
Remote and small, it came as a vision with trees
By a weaving stream, brushing the bank
With their violet shade, with somebody's limbs
Scattered among the matted, mildewed leaves nearby,
With his severed head rolling under the waves,
Breaking the shifting columns of light into a swirl
Of slivers and flecks; it came in a language
Untouched by pity, in a poem, lavish and dark,
Where death is reborn and sent into the world as a gift,
So the future, with no voice of its own, or hope
Of ever becoming more than it will be, might mourn.

from *The New Yorker*

Distance from Loved Ones

◇ ◇ ◇

After her husband died, Zita decided to get the face-lift she had always wanted. Half-way through the operation her blood pressure started to drop, and they had to stop. When Zita tried to fasten her seat-belt for her sad drive home, she threw out her shoulder. Back at the hospital the doctor examined her and found cancer run rampant throughout her shoulder and arm and elsewhere. Radiation followed. And, now, Zita just sits there in her beauty parlor, bald, crying and crying.

My mother tells me all this on the phone, and I say: Mother, who is Zita?

And my mother says, I am Zita. All my life I have been Zita, bald and crying. And you, my son, who should have known me best, thought I was nothing but your mother.

But, Mother, I say, I am dying. . . .

from *Denver Quarterly*

Aurora Borealis
and the Body Louse

◇   ◇   ◇

THE BODY LOUSE
    Today I feel altogether unbuttoned.
    I rejoice in these vast barrens of white
    And, you will understand, transform them
    In the expansive tracts of my genius.

AURORA BOREALIS
    If you were to try to flatter me
    With bardic vocables and sepia verse,
    I should object.

THE BODY LOUSE
                I think I shall sing,
    In a variety of forms, of light,
    Of sincerity, and of love, of course.

AURORA BOREALIS
    Oh, please. I don't give a shit for love.
    Fashion for me a desolate confection.
    I feel the need of a substantial torte,
    Lightly powdered with desperation.

THE BODY LOUSE
Bare elms under snow? The light falling
All afternoon? My large and tragic face
In the glass?

AURORA BOREALIS
I am no longer young.
My soul unravels as I contemplate
The man I loved in the naked presence
Of a beautiful woman, come upon
In silence and with joy.

THE BODY LOUSE
As in the dark
We are afraid? As we wake? Opening,
Again and again, our soft and empty hands?

AURORA BOREALIS
I cannot move. For the moment I am draped
In glacial distress. I can see the grand,
Groundless abyss under the dispassionate eye
Of vacant heaven. I can smell the nape
Of the neck of despair. It is coming to fasten me
In a tender embrace.

THE BODY LOUSE
How the mourning dove
Whistles, fatherless, from the trees?

AURORA BOREALIS
You know,
Love seemed the grandest plan of them all.
Perhaps the heart is simply too small.

THE BODY LOUSE
It may be. Though I can't really tell.
I find it hard to imagine the stark
Language of a large and foundering body.
What I see is an array of banks and streamers,
Patches of light, and hanging draperies.

AURORA BOREALIS
I will expand, I think, at the last, through the sadness.
See these slender rivers of ionospheric grief,
These noctilucent clouds and the vast desolation.

from *Grand Street*

ROSANNA WARREN

The Cormorant

◊   ◊   ◊

for Eunice

Up through the buttercup meadow the children lead
their father. Behind them, gloom
of spruce and fir, thicket through which they pried
into the golden ruckus of the field, toward home:

this rented house where I wait for their return
and believe the scene eternal. They have been out
studying the economy of the sea. They trudged to earn
sand-dollars, crab claws, whelk shells, the huge debt

repaid in smithereens along the shore:
ocean, old blowhard, wheezing in the give
and take, gulls grieving the shattered store.
It is your death I can't believe,

last night, inland, away from us, beyond
these drawling compensations of the moon.
If there's an exchange for you, some kind of bond,
it's past negotiation. You died alone.

Across my desk wash memories of ways
I've tried to hold you: that poem of years ago
starring you in your *mater dolorosa* phase;
or my Sunday picnic sketch in which the show

is stolen by your poised, patrician foot
above whose nakedness the party floats.
No one can hold you now. The point is moot.
I see you standing, marshalling your boats

of gravy, chutney, cranberry, at your vast
harboring Thanksgiving table, fork held aloft
while you survey the victualling of your coast.
We children surged around you, and you laughed.

Downstairs, the screen door slams, and slams me back
into the present, which you do not share.
Our children tumble in, they shake the pack
of sea-treasures out on table, floor, and chair.

But now we tune our clamor to your quiet.
The deacon spruces keep the darkest note
though hawkweed tease us with its saffron riot.
There are some wrecks from which no loose planks float,

nothing the sea gives back. I walked alone
on the beach this morning, watching a cormorant
skid, thudding, into water. It dove down
into that shuddering darkness where we can't

breathe. Impossibly long. Nothing to see.
Nothing but troughs and swells
over and over hollowing out the sea.
And, beyond the cove, the channel bells.

from *Boulevard*

A Wall in the Woods: Cummington

◇ ◇ ◇

I

What is it for, now that dividing neither
Farm from farm nor field from field it runs
Through deep impartial woods, and is transgressed
By boughs of pine or beech from either side?
Under that woven tester, buried here
Or there in laurel patch or shrouding vine,
It is for grief at what has come to nothing,
What even in this hush is scarcely heard—
Whipcrack, the ox's lunge, the stoneboat's grating,
Work shouts of young men stooped before their time,
Who in their stubborn heads foresaw forever
The rose of apples and the blue of rye.
It is for pride, as well, in pride that built
With levers, tackle, and abraded hands
What two whole centuries have not brought down.
Look how with shims they made the stones weigh
        inward,
Binding the water-rounded with the flat;
How to a small ravine they somehow lugged
A long, smooth girder of a rock, on which
To launch their wall in air, and overpass
The narrow stream that still slips under it.
Rosettes of lichen decorate their toils,

Who labored here like Pharaoh's Israelites;
Whose grandsons left for Canaans in the West.
Except to prompt a fit of elegy
It is for us no more, or if it is,
It is a sort of music for the eye,
A rugged ground-bass like the bagpipe's drone,
On which the leaf-light like a chanter plays.

II

He will hear no guff
About Jamshyd's court, this small,
Striped, duff-colored resident
On top of the wall,

Who, having given
An apotropaic shriek
Echoed by crows in heaven,
Is off like a streak.

There is no tracing
The leaps and scurries with which
He braids his long castle, ra-
Cing, by gap, ledge, niche

And Cyclopean
Passages, to reappear
Sentrylike on a rampart
Thirty feet from here.

What is he saying
Now, in a steady chipping
Succinctly plucked and cadenced
As water dripping?

It is not drum-taps
For a lost race of giants,
But perhaps says something, here
In Mr. Bryant's

Homiletic woods,
Of the brave art of forage
And the good of a few nuts
In burrow-storage;

Of agility
That is not sorrow's captive,
Lost as it is in being
Briskly adaptive;

Of the plenum, charged
With one life through all changes,
And of how we are enlarged
By what estranges.

from *The New Yorker*

Reading the Bible Backwards

◊　◊　◊

All around the altar, huge lianas
curled, unfurled the dark green
of their leaves to complement the red
of blood spilled there—a kind of Christmas
decoration, overhung with heavy vines
and over them, the stars.
When the angels came, messengers like birds
but with the oiled flesh of men, they hung
over the scene with smoldering swords,
splashing the world when they beat
their rain-soaked wings against the turning sky.

The child was bright in his basket
as a lemon, with a bitter smell from his wet
swaddling clothes. His mother bent
above him, singing a lullaby
in the liquid tongue invented
for the very young—short syllables
like dripping from an eave
mixed with the first big drops of rain
that fell, like tiny silver pears, from
the glistening fronds of palm. The three
who gathered there—old kings uncrowned:
the cockroach, condor and the leopard, lords
of the cracks below the ground, the mountain
pass and the grass-grown plain, were not
adorned, did not bear gifts, had not

come to adore; they were simply drawn
to gawk at this recurrent, awkward son
whom the wind had said would spell
the end of earth as it had been.

Somewhere north of this familiar scene
the polar caps were melting, the water was
advancing in its slow, relentless
lines, swallowing the old
landmarks, swelling the seas that pulled
the flowers and the great steel cities down.
The dolphins sport in the rising sea,
anemones wave their many arms like hair
on a drowned gorgon's head, her features
softened by the sea beyond all recognition.

On the desert's edge where the oasis dies
in a wash of sand, the sphinx seems to shift
on her haunches of stone, and the rain, as it runs down,
completes the ruin of her face. The Nile
merges with the sea, the waters rise
and drown the noise of earth. At the forest's
edge, where the child sleeps, the waters gather—
as if a hand were reaching for the curtain
to drop across the glowing, lit tableau.

When the waves closed over, completing the green
sweep of ocean, there was no time for mourning.
No final trump, no thunder to announce
the silent steal of waters; how soundlessly
it all went under: the little family
and the scene so easily mistaken
for an adoration. Above, more clouds poured in
and closed their ranks across the skies;
the angels, who had seemed so solid, turned
quicksilver in the rain.
                    Now, nothing but the wind
moves on the rain-pocked face

of the swollen waters, though far below
where giant squid lie hidden in shy tangles,
the whales, heavy-bodied as the angels,
their fins like vestiges of wings,
sing some mighty epic of their own—

a great day when the ships would all withdraw,
the harpoons fail of their aim, the land
dissolve into the waters, and they would swim
among the peaks of mountains, like eagles
of the deep, while far below them, the old
nightmares of earth would settle
into silt among the broken cities, the empty
basket of the child would float
abandoned in the seaweed until the work of water
unraveled it in filaments of straw,
till even that straw rotted
in the planetary thaw the whales prayed for,
sending their jets of water skyward
in the clear conviction they'd spill back
to ocean with their will accomplished
in the miracle of rain: *And the earth*
was without form and void, and darkness
was upon the face of the deep. And
the Spirit moved upon the face of the waters.

from *Sarah's Choice*

Saturday Morning Journal

◊ ◊ ◊

Nature, by nature, has no answers,
                    landscape the same.
Form tends toward its own dissolution.

There is an inaccessibility in the wind,
In the wind that taps the trees
With its white cane,
                    with its white cane and fingertips;
There is a twice-remove in the light
That falls,
          that falls like stained glass to the ground.

The world has been translated into a new language
Overnight, a constellation of signs and plain sense
I understand nothing of,
                    local objects and false weather
Out of the inborn,
As though I had asked for them, as though I had been there.

from *Antæus*

CONTRIBUTORS'
NOTES AND
COMMENTS

A. R. AMMONS was born in Whiteville, North Carolina, in 1926. He has taught at Cornell University since 1964. He has received the National Book Award (1973), the Bollingen Prize (1975), the National Book Critics Circle Award (1981), and a MacArthur Fellowship. He was lately elected a member of the Fellowship of Southern Writers. His most recent books are *The Selected Poems: Expanded Edition* and *Sumerian Vistas*, both published by Norton in 1987.

Of "The Damned," Ammons writes: "The writing of nature poetry is considered a pretty jaded activity in our time, a holdover or negative from the nineteenth century. Even so, I'm sure there were and are many kinds of nature poetry, and I hang on to one variable kind typical of my work throughout my writing life. My kind may not be mine alone—others may use the same stance—but I haven't studied others; I've merely tried to know my own way.

"It seems obvious to me that things and the world came first. In spite of all philosophical sophistry and negativism and subjectivism, I believe what's 'written' in the rocks. I believe that this planet is ancient, that it preceded man or manlike creatures by billions of years and preceded words and languages by at least an equal time. The center of consciousness for me is not verbal. I live in a world of things, not texts, not written texts. I feel that languages are arbitrary systems of intrinsic coherence and incoherence that arise, change, and disappear in response to circumstance, taking nothing from and adding nothing to nature. Our minds, the 'minds' of our predecessors, whether verbal, impressionistic, instinctive, or hormonal rose out of the creative forces of nature itself. Nature produced us. We were here with formed spines and backbones, with complex arterial systems, with enzymes and electrical charges long before we had names for any of it.

"So I feel deeply conditioned by nature. I expect to find, when I look at things around me, the sources of myself. But I don't go to nature for 'sermons in brooks' or for cute messages from rocks and weeds. Nature is not verbal. It is there. It comes first. I have found, though, that at times when I have felt charged with a vague energy or when I have moved into an intense consideration of what it means to be here, I sometimes by accident 'see' a structure or relationship in nature that clarifies the energy, releases it. Things are visible ideas. I recognize a correspondence, partial, of course, between my considerations and some configuration of things.

"In 'The Damned,' based, I imagine, on some photo of the Himalayan peaks, I found engaged my worry about what might be called 'innocent guilt,' something akin to but probably not the same thread as original sin. In the hierarchy of peaks the sainted summits, let's say, are not in spite of their height and purity innocent of the damnation of the lesser peaks, those that lack the majesty of thin air. We, as people, cannot be disentangled from the network of humanity, even though we have not intended to rise at the expense of others, and we are not free of an obligation to others, even if others are incapable of adding anything to us. I won't play out the disposition of the whole poem into exposition, except to note my dissatisfaction with the last line, which seems to me vulgar in its strong play. A quieter line is needed. And to say that the lower summits may have compensations of their own powerful enough to cast the highest summits as the damned.

"I don't say that nature gives me a complete text—or any textual analogy. But there are often configurations of things that surprisingly relate to and often clarify adumbrations we are daily swaying with."

JOHN ASH was born in Manchester, England, in 1948 and was educated at the University of Birmingham. Since 1985 he has lived in New York City. He has won grants and awards from the Ingram Merrill Foundation, the Whiting Foundation, and the Anne and Erlo Van Waveren Foundation. He has written reviews for the *Washington Post*, the *Village Voice*, and *Art in America*. His books include *The Goodbyes* (1982), *The Branching Stairs* (1984), and *Disbelief* (1987), all from Carcanet.

Of "The Sweeping Gesture," Ash writes: "The first few lines of the poem were the kind that arrive suddenly out of nowhere. The last two lines also achieved their final form very early on in the process. The rest of the poem proved much more difficult to write. "I can reveal that the hospital in question is St. Vincent's on Seventh Avenue in New York City, and that the poem was written during the sweltering summer of 1988 when I spent as much time as possible visiting friends in the country. The stanza in quotation marks describes Water Island. Other than that I think it's best to leave commentary to others."

JOHN ASHBERY was born in Rochester, New York, in 1927. He is the author of twelve books of poetry, including *April Galleons* (Viking, 1987). Twice named a Guggenheim Fellow, he received the Pulitzer Prize, the National Book Award, and the National Book Critics Circle Award for his 1975 collection, *Self-Portrait in a Convex Mirror* (Viking). A volume of his art criticism, *Reported Sightings*, was published in 1989 by Knopf. He delivered the Charles Eliot Norton lectures in poetry at Harvard University last year. He was guest editor of *The Best American Poetry 1988*.

MARVIN BELL was born in New York City in 1937; his hometown was Center Moriches, on eastern Long Island. He is the author of nine books of poetry, including *New and Selected Poems* (Atheneum, 1987) and *Iris of Creation* (Copper Canyon Press, 1990); a book of essays, *Old Snow Just Melting* (University of Michigan Press, 1983); and, with William Stafford, *Segues: A Correspondence in Poetry* (Godine, 1983). He has held a Guggenheim Fellowship and Senior Fulbright Appointments to Yugoslavia and Australia. He teaches at the University of Iowa, where he is Flannery O'Connor Professor of Letters, and lives part of each year in Port Townsend, Washington.

Bell writes: " 'Victim of Himself' seems to have found an extra portion of content through form and momentum and a lingering affection for the syllogism. With its O. Henry final act, the poem may have told a truth about conscience and happiness—or politics and love. Of course I didn't know, and wouldn't want to have known, what was coming when I began."

STEPHEN BERG was born in Philadelphia in 1934. He is Professor of English in the humanities department of the University of the Arts in Philadelphia and founder and co-editor of the *American Poetry Review*. His awards include a Guggenheim Fellowship, a grant from the National Endowment for the Arts, and the Frank O'Hara Memorial Prize from *Poetry* magazine. Recent books are *In It* (University of Illinois Press, 1986) and *Crow With No Mouth: Ikkyu* (Copper Canyon Press, 1989). A volume of new and selected poems is forthcoming from Copper Canyon in 1991. He is completing the third of three books—*Shaving, Porno Diva Numero Uno*, and *Oblivion*—whose forms explore the area between poetry and prose.

Berg writes: "Peter Haskell's translation of Bankei's 'Song of Original Mind,' published in his *Bankei Zen* (Grove Press, 1984), formed the basis of 'First Song.' I read his version endlessly; tired, irritable, helpless, listening to my mother ramble one afternoon, in the aftermath of a serious yearlong illness, for the greed of my own baffled ear I found myself beginning this vastly different poem. Much later the last three stanzas came, inspired by other Bankei pieces from the same wonderful book."

MEI-MEI BERSSENBRUGGE was born in Beijing, China, in 1947. She lives with her family in New Mexico and New York City. Her recent books are *The Heat Bird* (Burning Deck Press, 1984) and *Empathy* (Station Hill Press, 1989).

Berssenbrugge writes: "The location of 'Jealousy' is an apartment overlooking the reservoir in Central Park on New Year's Eve. I think about the reservoir often, because of its margins and changeable surface, even when frozen, due to warm currents underneath and the sunset light on it."

HAYDEN CARRUTH was born in Waterbury, Connecticut, in 1921. He teaches in the graduate creative writing program at Syracuse University. He has held, among others, two Guggenheim Fellowships and four NEA Fellowships. He has been appointed a Senior Fellow by the NEA. His most recent book is *Tell Me Again How the White Heron Rises and Flies Across the Nacreous River at Twilight Toward the Distant Islands* (New Directions, 1989).

Carruth writes: " 'Crucifixion' came to me quickly and easily on an autumn day in 1988. I simply wrote down what I saw either out my window or in my head."

ANNE CARSON was born in Toronto, Canada, in 1950. She is a professor of classics who has taught at the universities of Calgary, Toronto, Emory, Princeton, and McGill as well as at the 92nd Street Y in New York City where she was Rockefeller Scholar in Residence for 1986–87. She has published a study of love and hate titled *Eros the Bittersweet: An Essay* (Princeton University Press, 1986; repr. 1989) and a translation of Sophokles' *Elektra* (Oxford University Press, forthcoming). Current projects include an intellectual biography of the ancient Greek poet Simonides of Keos and a novel about Ray Charles.

Of "The Life of Towns," Carson writes: "The poem is part of an ongoing war with punctuation; we fought to a standstill here."

RAYMOND CARVER was born in Clatskanie, Oregon, in 1938. He died on August 2, 1988. His last book was *A New Path to the Waterfall* (Atlantic Monthly Press, 1989), a collection of poems. His fiction includes *Cathedral* (Vintage, 1984) and *Where I'm Calling From* (Atlantic Monthly Press, 1988). A Guggenheim Fellow in 1979, he received the Mildred and Harold Strauss living award in 1983, which allowed him to concentrate fully on his writing for the next five years. He was elected to the American Academy and Institute of Arts and Letters and was awarded a doctorate of letters from the University of Hartford. He also received the Brandeis Medal of Excellence for his fiction.

Tess Gallagher writes: "Reading 'Wake Up' a year and a half after my husband's death I'm amazed at how clearly the poem calls back that visit to Kyborg Castle outside Zurich the summer before Ray fell ill with lung cancer. Our friend, the critic and poet Harold Schweizer, had taken us to the castle and as we entered the torture chamber he expressed disappointment that we wouldn't be able to see the Iron Maiden because it was on tour somewhere. Nonetheless, Harold described it so vividly that Ray presents it here as if we had seen it, and we do see it in the poem. I recall that in early drafts the part about my pretending to wield an axe was not present. I reminded Ray of that as a complication that could show how those brutal gestures still inhabited the place so that the female character plays out the role of executioner as in some involuntary echo of the actual deaths that took place there. What had been done in play suddenly goes real and both man and woman feel the chill of it. The poem was written at a point when Ray could not pull back and avoid his own death, so this return to the site of a mock death, a death avoided or practiced, exists in tension with that unavoidable fate of our lives—that Ray was dying.

"The narrative brilliance of the poem should cause readers also to put their heads on the block with the speaker—then to experience that freshness which is life, is breath, is being able to walk free again into the light."

Tess Gallagher and Raymond Carver were companions for nearly eleven years. Shortly before his death they married in Reno in June 1988. She is a poet and short-story writer who currently holds the Willard and Lois Mackey Chair in Fiction at Beloit College. Her most recent book of poems is *Amplitude: New and Selected Poems* (Graywolf, 1987). The University of Michigan Press published her essays on poetry, *A Concert of Tenses*, in 1986.

AMY CLAMPITT was born at New Providence, Iowa, in 1920, graduated from Grinnell College, and has since lived mainly in New York City. Her books include *The Kingfisher* (1983), *What the Light Was Like* (1985), *Archaic Figure* (1987), and *Westward* (1990), all from Knopf. A Guggenheim Fellow in 1982–83, she has received the fellowship award for distinguished poetic achievement from the Academy of American Poets and is a member of the National Institute of Arts and Letters. She has been Writer in Residence at the College of William and Mary, Visiting Writer at Amherst College, and Visiting Hurst Professor at Washington University, as well as Phi Beta Kappa Poet at the Harvard Literary Exercises.

KILLARNEY CLARY was born in Los Angeles in 1953. Her chapbook, *By Me, By Any, Can and Can't Be Done*, was published by Greenhouse Review Press in 1980, and her first collection, *Who Whispered Near Me*, was published by Farrar, Straus & Giroux in 1989.

About the untitled poem beginning "Boys on street corners in Santa Ana . . ." Clary writes: "I wrote the poem a long time ago. I remember being distracted by the realization that there was something moving all the time—there is always water running somewhere. So the kids who sold the flowers and the people who started their days when I finished mine had an empty mystery for me. There was so much happening to them that I could never know."

ROBERT CREELEY was born in Arlington, Massachusetts, in 1926. At Black Mountain College, where he taught between 1954 and 1956, he established and edited *Black Mountain Review*. Recent and forthcoming publications include his *Selected Poems* (University of California Press), *Windows* (New Directions, 1990), and his edition of *The Essential Burns* (Ecco Press, 1989). At the State University of New York at Buffalo, where he has taught since 1966, he is SUNY Distinguished Professor and Samuel P. Capen Professor of Poetry and the Humanities. He has received the Walt Whitman Citation of Merit as New York State Poet (1989–91).

Creeley writes that "Thinking" was "writ in Helsinki, and somewhat prompted by Donald Hall saying I might satisfy a longtime irritation with Harvard by publishing insistently poems in their journal (my plan, not his). Anyhow I had this thought of how habituated and meager are finally the conscious determinations of one's life—at least in that frame of the well secured, now dozing instance. It otherwise got writ as most things I write, with one shift of line later (thanks to Don's reading), having to do with the form of water, etc. Well, back to sleep (which is what one tended to do in Finland)."

CHRISTOPHER DAVIS was born in Whittier, California, in 1960. He teaches creative writing at the University of North Carolina at Charlotte. His first book, *The Tyrant of the Past and the Slave of the Future*, won the 1988 AWP Award in Poetry (it was chosen by Gerald Stern) and was published by Texas Tech University Press in 1989. New work received the 1989 poetry award from *Sonora Review*. He received an MFA from the Writers' Workshop at the University of Iowa in 1985, where he was a Teaching-Writing Fellow.

Of "Dying in Your Garden of Death to Go Back into My Garden," Davis writes: "I wrote this poem during a difficult time. The friend I was living with and I were working at lousy jobs all the time, had no money, and were no longer capable of soothing each other. On weekends, I could think of only two ways to use my time: I lurked around Golden Gate Park, and I wrote. Sometimes I'd bring a book. I felt isolated, irresponsible, dispossessed, mad. I felt I had to write poetry in which language turned self-destructiveness outward from the self, externalized it. Whatever the consequences. I had to feel alive."

TOM DISCH was born in Des Moines, Iowa, in 1940. He is the author of *Yes, Let's: New and Selected Poems* (Johns Hopkins, 1989) and of many works of fiction, including *334*, *On Wings of Song*, and, in collaboration with Charles Naylor, *Neighboring Lives* (Scribner's, 1981). He has been *The Nation's* theater critic since 1987. In 1989 his adaptation of *Ben Hur* was presented by the RAPP Theater Company in Baltimore and New York. He lives in New York City.

Disch writes: "I wrote 'The Crumbling Infrastructure' in September 1986, having recently returned to New York City from a rustic cabin in the Catskills, not far from the Delaware River, where I had been one of the capsized canoeists noted in the poem. The toing and froing from country to city kept me alert to what the two realms have in common, and the poem probably takes most of its energy from that alternating current."

NORMAN DUBIE was born in Barre, Vermont, in 1945. He is the author of more than a dozen volumes of poetry. He has received fellowships from the Guggenheim Foundation, the Ingram Merrill Foundation, and the National Endowment for the Arts. His most recent collection of poems, *Groom Falconer*, was published by Norton in 1989. He teaches at Arizona State University in Tempe, Arizona.

Dubie writes: " 'Of Politics, & Art' began in draft and was abandoned. Years later it was taken up again, still just a memory of childhood, but something new had insinuated itself upon the poem—this new element was a fragment of dialogue that had drifted up a long hallway to me a week before. It altered the course of the original poem somewhat, and gave the poem its title. The reader will probably need to be reminded, as the poet was, that the word *rendering* applies to fat and whaling as well as to the nineteenth-century kit of chalk pastels. The poem, oddly enough, is absolutely accurate in its treatment of an experience from childhood. It is an homage to a great teacher."

AARON FOGEL was born in the Bronx, New York, in 1947. He lives in Cambridge, Massachusetts, with his wife and son and teaches at Boston University. His books include *Chain Hearings* (Inwood/Horizon, 1976) and *Coercion to Speak: Conrad's Poetics of Dialogue* (Harvard University Press, 1985). He has published essays and poems in *Raritan* and *Western Humanities Review*. A Guggenheim Fellow in 1987, he has a couple of comic novels in progress. His work was included in the 1989 edition of *The Best American Poetry*.

Of "The Chessboard Is on Fire," Fogel writes: "The oracular ant, the demographic priest, the censor-provost, the Isle of Lewis ivory chesspieces, the ceramist, the lettuce head, the chessmaster, and the other figures in the poem are meant to be seriocomic abstract characters. The demographic priest, for example, whoever he is, happens to come from critical work I've been at on the history of the image of poets as corrective or better census-takers, count-fixers—the utopian fantasy of poetry's subtler measures and rhythms and counts as somehow corrective to what's wrong or unjust or oversimplified in social measurement—but no one could know that, and I hope it's not important that anyone does now. One polysyllable not in the poem is catachresis: getting into poetry the dismissive, contemptuous, embittered sounds in colloquial speech I feel I grew up with (but perhaps it was only me), as in the by now banal 'shm' prefix to words. Even in the exclamation points in the poem I wanted to register different proportions and degrees of crude skepticism and dismissiveness, as well as clamor or hope. The line about reading Yiddish well, for example, is not an exclamation of simple aspiration, at least I hope it's not, but of impossibility or disbelief, in what is itself a dismissive or skeptically post-Yiddish tone, comically referring back to the poem's own mixed commitment to its lamentable obscurity. The word *apocussion* I wanted to suggest not an apocalypse but a percussive sound going away from the listener."

JAMES GALVIN was born in Chicago in 1951. He teaches one semester a year at the University of Iowa and spends the rest of the year on the Colorado–Wyoming border. He has received grants from the National Endowment for the Arts, the Ingram Merrill Foundation, and the John Simon Guggenheim Memorial Foundation. His books are *Imaginary Timber* (Doubleday, 1980), *God's Mistress* (Harper & Row, 1984), and *Elements* (Copper Canyon Press, 1988).

Galvin writes: " 'To the Republic' was written for my friend Ray Worster, who was born on Boulder Ridge in 1918 and froze to death there in 1984."

SUZANNE GARDINIER was born in New Bedford in 1961 and grew up in Scituate, Massachusetts. She graduated from the University of Massachusetts in 1981 and from the Columbia University MFA program in 1986. She teaches and lives in Sag Harbor, where she is at work on a book-length poem called "The New World." Her work was included in the 1989 edition of *The Best American Poetry*.

Gardinier writes: " 'This Land' was written in 1986. It is part of a manuscript called *The Gathering of Intelligence*."

AMY GERSTLER was born in San Diego, California, in 1956. She teaches English and writing at UCLA Extension and Otis/Parsons. In 1987 she won second prize in *Mademoiselle* magazine's fiction contest. Her most recent book of poems is *Bitter Angel* (North Point Press, 1990).

Gerstler writes: " 'The Ice Age' was my attempt to counterpoint various obsessions I've had since childhood (the Ice Age, the symbolic content of snow and cold, cave painting, avalanches and other natural disasters, and science laboratories) with a mounting sense of fear and helplessness about two things that grieve me much in adult life: mankind's fatal befouling of the earth in the name of progress, and the AIDS epidemic."

LINDA GREGG was born in Suffern, New York, in 1942. She received her BA and MA degrees at San Francisco State University. She is the author of *Too Bright to See* (Graywolf Press, 1981) and *Alma* (Random House, 1985) and has received a Guggenheim Fellowship and a Whiting Writer's Award. She spent six months in Nicaragua and wrote "The War" while she was there.

THOM GUNN was born in Gravesend, England, in 1929. He has lived in California since 1954. His most recent publications are *Selected Poems* (1979) and *The Passages of Joy* (1982), both from Farrar, Straus & Giroux. His book of essays, *The Occasions of Poetry*, was published in 1982 by Faber and Faber in London.

Of "Duncan," Gunn writes: "Here is some annotation, for those who want it. I think the poem Robert Duncan was writing on the ferry was 'Heavenly City, Earthly City,' and the year in that case was 1946. He gave his last poetry reading, the one referred to in this poem, on the Berkeley campus early in 1986. The references toward the end of the poem are to H.D.'s *Hermetic Definition* and to the Venerable Bede."

DONALD HALL was born in New Haven, Connecticut, in 1928. He lives in New Hampshire where he makes his living by free-lance writing. In 1990 he published *Anecdotes of Modern Art* (Oxford University Press), *Old and New Poems* and *Letter from Eagle Pond* (both from Ticknor & Fields), and *The Essential Andrew Marvell* (Ecco Press). *The One Day* (Ticknor & Fields, 1988) won the National Book Critics Circle Award for poetry. Hall was guest editor of *The Best American Poetry 1989*.

Of "Praise for Death," Hall writes: "In the autumn of 1980 I wrote some lines under the provisional title of 'Psalms,' which were the beginning of this poem. Maybe a liturgical tone remains in some lines. I gathered material for a few years, and did most of the writing between 1984 and 1988. 'Praise for Death' overlapped with *The One Day*, especially with work on 'Four Classic Texts' —the common mode is relentlessness—and this five-line stanza derives from the ten-line stanza of *The One Day*. Here, it's mostly a visual grid within which to juxtapose diverse materials. After working on this poem for a long time, I remembered *Gilgamesh's* terrible lamentation; I added the King of Uruk to the beginning of the poem and a paraphrase for the ending. "This poem takes its structure from its method of composition. It could only be written over a long period, with amalgamations, rewritings, reorganizations, and connections dreamed-out after years of staring at it. Other poems depend on a piece of luck, they may be *there* in one quick take—even though they take a long time to finish. A poem like 'Praise for Death' constructs itself adding phrase to phrase like grains of sand accumulating a hill."

DANIEL HALPERN was born in Syracuse, New York, in 1945. He is the author of six collections of poetry, including *Tango, Seasonal Rights*, and *Life Among Others*, all published by Viking Penguin, and is editor of *Antæus* and the Ecco Press. He has edited *The American Poetry Anthology* (Avon, 1975), *The Art of the Tale: An International Anthology of Short Stories* (Viking Penguin, 1986), and *Writers on Artists* and *On Nature*, both from North Point Press. He is co-author of a cookbook, *The Good Food: Soups, Stews, and Pastas* (Viking Penguin, 1985), and recently published a travel book, *Halpern's Guide to the Essential Restaurants of Italy* (Addison-Wesley, 1990). His awards include a Guggenheim Fellowship and a grant from the National Endowment for the Arts. He teaches in the graduate writing program of Columbia University.

Of "Bell & Capitol," Halpern writes: "This seems to me—although I should rightly be the last to know for sure—to be an atypical poem in the context of my other work. It comes from a source unknown to me, but reading it I imagine I had a number of locations pushing the poem forward: Cavafy's Alexandria, a forgotten Roman port town, certain paintings from the Italian Renaissance, a fictional incident involving the Spanish armada, or perhaps, most simply, a mythological place located by that part of the unconscious that houses forgotten impressions."

ROBERT HASS was born in San Francisco in 1941. He is the author of *Field Guide* (Yale University Press, 1973), *Praise* (Ecco Press, 1979), and *Human Wishes* (Ecco, 1989). He has also published a book of essays, *Twentieth-Century Pleasures: Prose on Poetry* (Ecco, 1984), which won the National Book Critics Circle Award for criticism. He teaches at the University of California, Berkeley.

Hass writes: "The title of 'Berkeley Eclogue' probably has much to do with the sound *kl*, but 'eclogue' also suggested the stylization in poetry of a certain dynamic of thinking through another voice or other voices, in this case interior ones. No shepherds in Berkeley, though parenting belongs in some ways to the pastoral metaphor."

SEAMUS HEANEY was born in Northern Ireland in 1939. Currently he teaches one semester a year at Harvard University. His most recent books are *The Government of the Tongue* (1988) and *The Haw Lantern* (1987), both from Farrar, Straus & Giroux. In 1989, he was elected Professor of Poetry at Oxford University.

Of "Crossings," Heaney writes: "In the autumn of 1988 I began to write twelve-line poems in groups of twelve—little skimmings and glances and sallies. The motif behind these pieces is that of passage from one place or state to another."

ANTHONY HECHT was born in New York City in 1923. He is currently University Professor at Georgetown University. He has received the Pulitzer Prize, the Bollingen Prize, and the Eugenio Montale Award. His books include *A Summoning of Stones* (Macmillan, 1954), *The Hard Hours* (Atheneum, 1967), *Millions of Strange Shadows* (Atheneum, 1977), *The Venetian Vespers* (Atheneum, 1979), and *The Transparent Man* (Knopf, 1990). Knopf published Hecht's *Collected Earlier Poems* in 1990.

Of "Eclogue of the Shepherd and the Townie," Hecht writes: "I enjoyed writing this 'debate-poem,' which derives from such earlier practitioners as Virgil, Marvell, and Frost. The poem is also meant, in a slightly more covert way, as homage to Stevens and Auden. The vituperations of the first two speeches are perhaps too symmetrically balanced by the 'positive' claims of the second two, but they are all part of an unresolvable puzzle about notions of 'innocence' and 'virtue' that extend over the entire range of human behavior from the pastoral, conservative, know-nothing, Luddite suspicion of anything 'cultivated' to the dandified, academic, book-learning, theoretical meliorist's distrust of the 'primitive.' "

EMILY HIESTAND was born in Chicago in 1947 and grew up in Oak Ridge, Tennessee. She is a poet and visual artist, and creative co-director of The Artemis Ensemble, whose performances explore the languages of sustainable habitation. She received a BFA from the Philadelphia College of Art, an MA from the Writing Program of Boston University, and is completing a Ph.D. in poetics and philosophy of nature in the University Professors Program of Boston University. In 1988 her poetry received the *Nation*'s Discovery award and her first book, *Green the Witch-Hazel Wood* (Graywolf Press, 1989), was selected by Jorie Graham for the National Poetry Series. Her essays and poems have appeared in *The Nation, The Atlantic, The Hudson Review, Prairie Schooner, The Boston Review, Salmagundi, Kalliope Journal, The Boston Globe Magazine,* and other publications. A second book, *The Idea of Home,* is forthcoming.

Emily Hiestand writes: " 'On Nothing' was provoked one Sunday morning by a newspaper commentary on the plays and ideas of Samuel Beckett. Only recently had I begun to realize, from the poetry of William Wordsworth and Richard Wilbur, that one could make a line with a long, open pulse, and that one could twine lyrical and philosophical language, intuition and logic: the image I had was of the double helix strands of the DNA model made by Watson and Crick: strands that turn in tandem around a central axis, yet remain distinct, and suggest, by their linear curvature, a sculptural, open, and permeable volume. That morning, the two strands began to sustain themselves, precariously, an event that recalled nothing so much as the unforgettable moment that the bicycle balances, and one moves, more quickly now, out into a partially known, partially unknown neighborhood.

"That morning was in 1984, early in my encounter with poetry, and I had not quite yet learned to recognize the sensation at the fringe of consciousness that announces an unexpected poem. Several times, imagining that I had made some notes for a would-be conversation with Mr. Beckett, I returned to the Sunday news, only to have the peculiar sensation tug again. Not all poems arrive this way, but that morning, poetry taught me to notice, to yield to, and to sustain one form of arrival.

"Here too, language began to suggest a metaphysics and epistemology that found its figures in the homely imagery of the 1950s South. To find that the cosmic mysteries of Before-life and After-life, familiar to me from orthodox Eastern and Christian religious imagery, resolved themselves into the skewers on summer corn, was a plainness before which I could only surrender with a smile. In a self-reflexive way, the language of this poem began to probe into the known and unknown region of a particular past, of memory, and into the 'nameless quarter,' some 'thing beyond reckoning.' As it did so, an enduring intuition emerged: that human consciousness is 'emitted from nature like shad roe, oxides, uranium and burls,' that we are, in our capacity to imagine fullness and emptiness, so far from being alien on it, a principle from within the earth being. The question and proposal of this poem have proved to be my primary, ongoing exploration. Now, I should think that the view of consciousness arrived at in this poem would render our species more, rather than less, responsible within the earth. Perhaps, in time, we will become so adept within being that we, in the way proposed by the Tao Te Ching, do nothing."

BRENDA HILLMAN was born in Tucson, Arizona, in 1951. She was educated at Pomona College and at the University of Iowa. Since 1976 she has resided in the San Francisco Bay Area. Her first book, *White Dress* (Wesleyan University Press, 1985), received the Delmore Schwartz Memorial Award and the Norma Farber First Book Award from the Poetry Society of America. Her second book, *Fortress*, was published by Wesleyan in 1989. She has received a National Endowment for the Arts fellowship. She teaches at St. Mary's College in Moraga, California. "No Greener Pastures" initially appeared in *Quarry West*.

Of "No Greener Pastures," Hillman writes: "This poem was written in 1984 when I had just started teaching composition at St. Mary's College, a small Catholic college in the green hills of the suburbs. I was both delighted and amused by the process of teaching language at such a basic level. And learning language at all seemed, suddenly, a heart-breakingly moving struggle, and also very funny. I wanted to capture the experiences of learning to teach and write, *and* of learning to commute, and of learning what can and cannot be 'represented' by language. This is also a poem in which I was very conscious of using the simile as a device to heighten irony and to make surprises."

JOHN HOLLANDER was born in New York City in 1929 and is currently A. Bartlett Giamatti Professor of English at Yale. He has been awarded the Bollingen and Levinson prizes for his many books of poetry and criticism, the most recent of which are *Harp Lake* (Knopf, 1988) and *Melodious Guile: Fictive Pattern in Poetic Language* (Yale University Press, 1988).

Hollander writes: " 'An Old-Fashioned Song' was written in response to a request for some verse for adults who had recently learned to read; it was to have short lines and syntax that wasn't too demanding. I started out with a version of the first line of Théodore de Banville's well-known *'Nous n'irons plus au bois, / Les lauriers sont coupés,'* and simply let the resonance of that line, and its desire to return as a refrain, take it from there. The turn on 'they are gone for good, and you for ill' may in fact have been elusive for some of the intended readers, but perhaps not."

VIRGINIA HOOPER was born in Marianna, Florida, in 1955. She grew up in Pensacola, Florida, before moving north to study photojournalism at Boston University. She received her undergraduate degree from Harvard, where she studied art history, and her MFA from Columbia, where she was a Merit Fellow in poetry. She has worked as a fiction editor for *Penthouse International* and as a research associate for *Vanity Fair*. She has taught children's poetry workshops at Rusk Institute for Rehabilitative Medicine, has painted and exhibited in New York City, and is a co-editor of *American Letters & Commentary*.

Of "Climbing Out of the Cage," Hooper writes: "Rarely have I written in a dramatic voice, if you could call this voice dramatic. I discovered the character Blue Dog in an actor's workshop. We were instructed, through written exercises and physical enactments, to uncover a personality that would gradually emerge from the various angles of perspective. For instance, I had to embody the way Blue Dog walked, I had to answer a lengthy list of questions regarding Blue Dog's circumstances of birth, I had to examine her sadness and the environment in which she had come to live. Only later was I able to understand what kept her alive, what her project entailed. I still see her very much as a Beckett character (perhaps a cousin)—stripped of concrete locale, centered in an abstract space of contemplation, though one of strange beauty and sensual presence. An abstract painting."

RICHARD HOWARD was born in Cleveland in 1929. He has published over 150 translations from the French, including Baudelaire's complete *Les Fleurs du mal* (Godine, 1982), for which he received the American Book Award for translation. In 1970 he won the Pulitzer Prize for his third book of poems, *Untitled Subjects* (Atheneum, 1969). Subsequent collections include *Two-Part Inventions* (1974), *Misgivings* (1979), and *Lining Up* (1984), all from Atheneum, and *No Traveller* (Knopf, 1989). "The Victor Vanquished" will appear in a forthcoming volume, *Elegies, Etc.* (Knopf). Howard is at work on a new translation of Proust's *In Search of Lost Time*.

Of "The Victor Vanquished," Howard writes: "The last two years of his life before he died of AIDS, Tom Victor, the photographer and former collaborator of the poet, withdrew from his friends and died in silence and solitude in Detroit. The poem is an attempt to come to terms with such a cancellation of the usual ties of human community."

FANNY HOWE was born in Buffalo, New York, in 1940. She is Professor of Literature at the University of California, San Diego. She has won a grant from the NEA and a MacDowell Colony Fellowship, and is a Fellow of the Bunting Institute. Her most recent publications include *The Vineyard* (Lost Roads Press, 1988), *The Deep North* (Sun and Moon Books, 1988), and *Famous Questions* (Available Press, 1988).

Of "Perfection and Derangement," Howe writes: "The poem is part of a series exploring hells on earth. From each one comes one voice or many, representing speech from the spirit-world. I think the perspective behind them could be called Gnostic."

RODNEY JONES was born in Falkville, Alabama, in 1950. He is the author of three books of poetry: *The Story They Told Us of Light* (University of Alabama Press, 1980), *The Unborn* (Atlantic Monthly Press, 1985), and *Transparent Gestures* (Houghton Mifflin, 1989). In 1989 he received the Jean Stein Award from the American Academy and Institute of Arts and Letters and the Award for Literary Excellence in Poetry from *The Kenyon Review*. He teaches English at Southern Illinois University at Carbondale. *Transparent Gestures* won the National Book Critics Circle Award for poetry in 1990.

Of "On the Bearing of Waitresses," Jones writes: "Initially, I had in mind a sort of poem that would recognize waitresses as an unacknowledged but ancient and important religious order. I intended to show them as individual embodiments of archetypal figures, but the images of the waitresses I had known kept drawing me back into the peculiarities of their own individual situations. Eventually, the poem became a quarrel between the typifying mind and the mind that recognizes singularity. The waitress who picks up the speaker at the end of the poem, for all her idiosyncrasies, is preferable to a type."

GALWAY KINNELL teaches in the creative writing program at New York University. He was recently named state poet of Vermont. "When One Has Lived a Long Time Alone" is the title poem of a new collection to be published in the fall of 1990.

EDWARD KLEINSCHMIDT was born in Winona, Minnesota, in 1951. He teaches creative writing at Santa Clara University. His second collection of poems, *First Language* (which includes "Gangue"), won the 1989 Juniper Prize (University of Massachusetts Press, 1990). In 1987 the Heyeck Press published a limited letterpress edition of his first book of poems, *Magnetism*, which won the 1988 Poetry Award from the San Francisco Bay Area Book Reviewers Association. He has published poems in *The New Yorker, The American Poetry Review, Poetry, The Gettysburg Review*, and *Denver Quarterly*. He lives in San Francisco.

Kleinschmidt writes: "I wrote 'Gangue' in Il Cedro, a house that the poet Frances Mayes and I rented in the summer of 1987. We knew the house would be much too big for us, but we wanted to live in the Mugello, the area north of Florence. The nearest town was Vicchio, the birthplace of Giotto, and right down an unpaved road was the famous bridge where Cimabue had discovered the young Giotto drawing a perfect sheep in the dirt. 'Gangue' is one of six poems I wrote in a large dark room off the hall. Rereading the poems, I discovered how influenced I was by the immensity and strangeness of the house itself. The kitchen had place settings for eighty. We opened a creaking door upstairs one day and discovered an entire wing to the house no one had lived in for years. In the drawers were stacks of invitations and birth announcements for 1953 and 1961. Olga, the seventy-five-year-old caretaker, lived in another wing, and she would come flying in whenever the high winds of the summer storms would slam the heavy wooden shutters in the house, and she would close them all, and darken the entire house.

"I started 'Gangue' one morning while reading an old dictionary. The page with the word *gangue* fell out of the dictionary onto the cool tile floor. I hadn't seen the word before but felt it obliquely fit the contents and aura of the house: 'The worthless rock or other material in which valuable minerals are found.' While interwoven in the poem are statements and images of my experiences that summer, most of the lines and words refer to the title and are somewhat elegiac: only half the clocks in the cars work, the graffiti-covered floor of Siena's Duomo is covered with boards to protect the graffiti. The laryngectomy I mention is Remo's, the owner of a small grocery store in the small village, Montisi, not far from Pienza. Most of the lines refer to fragmentation, useless motions, the flat sequence of habit, all encased, all overwhelmed by the energy of the 'valuable minerals' in the vein, the vibrancy of summer in Italy, the continuity of the centuries-old stone bridge where a boy drew a sheep in the sand."

YUSEF KOMUNYAKAA was born in Bogalusa, Louisiana, in 1947. He is the author of *Copacetic* (1984), *I Apologize for the Eyes in My Head* (1986), and *Dien Cai Dau* (1989), all from Wesleyan University Press. He teaches in the creative writing program and in Afro-American studies at Indiana University, and lives in Bloomington. In 1969 and 1970 he served with the Army in Vietnam.

Komunyakaa writes: " 'Facing It' attempts to capture the pathos of the war through the reflective power of the Vietnam Veterans' Memorial in Washington, D.C. The journey is from the external terrain to an internal one."

DENISE LEVERTOV was born in London, England, in 1923. *A Door in the Hive* (New Directions, 1989) is her latest book of poetry. She lives in Seattle and teaches at Stanford University every winter.

Of "Ikon: The Harrowing of Hell," Levertov writes: "I have long been fascinated by the tradition that Christ, in the interval between His death on the cross and His resurrection, descended into limbo to rescue the souls of the innocent and just who had died before His birth. Didmas was the 'good thief' crucified on a neighboring cross, to whom Jesus promised that 'today thou shalt be with me in paradise.' The harrowing of hell is the subject of many medieval paintings and of many Greek and Russian ikons."

PHILIP LEVINE was born in Detroit in 1928. He has been writing poetry for over forty years and is now preparing his fourteenth book of poems for publication; the book, *What Work Is*, will be published by Knopf in 1991. His most recent volume, *A Walk with Tom Jefferson*, won the Bay Area Book Reviewers Award for poetry published in 1988. His books have also won the National Book Critics Circle Award, the American Book Award, and the Lenore Marshall Prize. In 1987 he received the Ruth Lilly Award given by the Modern Poetry Association and the American Council for the Arts "in recognition of outstanding poetic achievement." After teaching for seven years at Tufts he has returned to Fresno State to finish his teaching career in a public school among his peers.

Of "Scouting," Levine writes: "In 1954 I went to Boone, North Carolina, to marry Frances Artley (who is still—thank God—my wife). She had a job there costuming a summer play called *Horn in the West*, & I had just given up my last grease-shop job in Detroit, so I had time to walk among the hills and fields and mountainsides. For much of a summer I lived close to nature, and I discovered the rural poor of the South on their own turf. I'd known many of them as fellow students & fellow workers in Detroit, & now I saw the world they'd fled because it has failed to feed them. Except for their hideous racism, they were the most considerate and generous people I had ever met. I remember them often, and one morning in the fall of '87 while living in Somerville, Massachusetts, I felt welling up in me the old hatred for what America has done to its good people, for I was seeing the human cost of Reaganomics every day on the streets of Somerville, Medford, and Boston. I wanted to feel otherwise about my country, so once again I took an imaginative voyage back in time to try to rediscover the people who helped make my life worth living."

THOMAS LUX was born in Massachusetts in 1946. A 1988 recipient of a Guggenheim Fellowship, he teaches at Sarah Lawrence College. He has held National Endowment for the Arts fellowships three times. His most recent book is *The Drowned River* (Houghton Mifflin, 1990).

NATHANIEL MACKEY was born in Miami, Florida, in 1947. He is the author of *Eroding Witness* (University of Illinois Press, 1985), a National Poetry Series selection, and *Bedouin Hornbook* (Callaloo Fiction Series, 1986). He edits the literary magazine *Hambone* and teaches at the University of California, Santa Cruz.

KEVIN MAGEE was born in Miami, Florida, in 1957. He moved to Iowa in 1980. His poems have appeared in *Another Chicago Magazine*, *The Antioch Review*, *B City*, *Caliban*, *New American Writing*, and issues of *Ploughshares* edited by Thomas Lux and Bill Knott. New work is in *Tyuonyi*.

Magee writes: "Some of the motivating pressures around the writing of 'Road' might be identified with my reading of Louis Zukofsky's *A-8* and *A-9*, to which I was introduced in the course of several talks given by Michael Palmer in Iowa City in 1986. The notational character of much of the writing in *A-8* was as instructive an example as the text's proximity to writings by Marx and Lenin. The sectioning used by George Oppen in *Of Being Numerous* and, especially, in *Route* helped suggest a sequential pattern or form. I had a job in industry during the time of the writing (driving a forklift in a meatpacking plant) and so was in a position to participate, however marginally, in some of the marches and rallies and related protest events organized by slaughterhouse workers in response to repeated attacks by corporations and the government on their wages and way of life. The extent to which this order of experience (proletarian?) can be inscribed by the lyric onto Time, 'the times,' may be one question the poem intends to ask. Whitman wrote in an early notebook: 'I will not descend among professors and capitalists—I will turn the ends of my trousers around my boots, and my cuffs back from my wrists, and go with drivers and boatmen and men that catch fish or work in the field.' "

THOMAS MCGRATH was born on a North Dakota farm in 1916. He was a Rhodes Scholar at New College, Oxford, and served in the Air Force in the Aleutians during World War II. He received a Guggenheim Fellowship in 1968 and a National Endowment for the Arts Senior Fellowship in 1987. His *Selected Poems: 1938–1988* (Copper Canyon Press, 1988) was nominated for the National Book Critics Circle Award and won the Lenore Marshall/*Nation* Poetry Prize in 1989.

LYNNE MCMAHON was born in Iowa in 1951. She currently teaches at the University of California, Irvine. She has received an Ingram Merrill Award and a Missouri Arts Council grant. Her book *Faith* was published by Wesleyan University Press in 1988. She has just completed a new manuscript, tentatively titled *Devolution of the Nude*.

Of "Barbie's Ferrari," McMahon writes: "Barbie's first car was a Corvette—racy, glamorous, American-made—which seemed appropriate, an upper-class daredeviltry that nevertheless managed to stay local. It was conceivable, for instance, that Barbie could drive this car to the malt shop (the Midwest or Southern Barbie) or the beach (the L.A. freeway Barbie) or across the Triborough Bridge (the New York shopping Barbie). Her car was recognizably American; I thought that was the point. So I was a bit surprised when Barbie's Ferrari appeared ('Oh, yes,' my five-year-old said knowledgeably, ' "a red hot dream" '). This had jet-set written all over it, and we all know what that means. Empty affairs, estrangement, pills, the downward spiral of lost innocence. This could signal the beginning of the end, the Monte Carlo Barbie, the Greek shipping magnate Barbie, alone on the Autobahn and far from home."

JANE MEAD was born in Baltimore, Maryland, in 1958. She attended Vassar College, Syracuse University, and the University of Iowa, and now lives in Napa, California. Her poems have appeared in

The Virginia Quarterly Review, Ploughshares, Ironwood, Pequod, and other magazines.

Mead writes: "When I wrote 'Concerning That Prayer I Cannot Make,' I'd been trying to write a poem that was really *about* this poem. Finally, frustrated, I went out for a walk and to sit by the river, under the railway bridge near where I lived—which I did a lot that winter. And there I just wrote what I really wanted to say, which was this poem. I think this kind of experience is common; I *know* that I easily forget what I learned by it. Now, when a poem isn't going well, I try to remember to ask myself, 'Well, what do you *really* mean?' and sometimes that helps get me to that moment when you quit *creating* and just go with the deeper *saying* of it."

JAMES MERRILL was born in New York City in 1926. He received his BA from Amherst College in 1947 and published his *First Poems* in 1951 (Knopf). His books have received two National Book Awards, the Pulitzer Prize, and the Bollingen Prize in poetry. The epic poem begun in *Divine Comedies* (Atheneum, 1976) and extended in two subsequent volumes was published in its entirety as *The Changing Light at Sandover* (1983), which won the National Book Critics Circle Award. His most recent books are *Late Settings* (Atheneum, 1985) and *The Inner Room* (Knopf, 1988). He divides his time between Stonington, Connecticut, and Key West, Florida.

W. S. MERWIN was born in New York City in 1927 and grew up in Union City, New Jersey, and in Scranton, Pennsylvania. From 1949 to 1951 he worked as a tutor in France, Portugal, and Majorca. After that, for several years he made the greater part of his living by translating from French, Spanish, Latin, and Portuguese. His books of poetry include *A Mask for Janus* (Yale University Press, 1952); *The Moving Target* (Atheneum, 1963); *The Carrier of Ladders* (Atheneum, 1970), for which he won the Pulitzer Prize; *The Compass Flower* (Atheneum, 1977); and *The Rain in the Trees* (Knopf, 1988). His *Selected Translations 1948–1968* (Atheneum) won the PEN Translation Prize in 1968. In 1987 he received the Governor's Award for Literature of the State of Hawaii. Atheneum published his *Selected Poems* in 1988.

JANE MILLER was born in New York City in 1949. She is now with the Creative Writing Program at the University of Arizona in Tucson. She has been awarded a fellowship from the Guggenheim Foundation as well as grants from the National Endowment for the Arts and the Vermont Council on the Arts. Her books of poetry include *American Odalisque*, from Copper Canyon Press (1988), which won the inaugural Four Corners Book Award in Poetry and was nominated for *The Los Angeles Times* Book Award; a collaboration in the prose poem with Olga Broumas, *Black Holes, Black Stockings* (Wesleyan University Press, 1985); and *The Greater Leisures* (Doubleday, 1983), which won the National Poetry Series Open Competition.

Miller writes: " 'Adoration' is a 'reading' of our culture. I attempted to make the language subversive, raw, and intense in describing a sample evening of contemporary American life. The poem is both narrative and lyrical. I also attempt to undercut the narration and lyricism in lines syntactically awry. Yet the poem is stabilized, I think, by both the title and the motility of the language. I wanted to see if I could get a reader to embrace the dissociation in our lives and to be moved by the challenge of these accelerated times. The self wanders through the poem as an agent, and representative, of the images."

SUSAN MITCHELL was conceived in the warm waters of the Atlantic off southeast Florida, or possibly onshore in an art deco hotel, but grew up in New York City. She is a graduate of Wellesley College and holds a master's degree from Georgetown University. *The Water Inside the Water*, a collection of her poems, was published by Wesleyan University Press in 1983. She has been a fellow of the Fine Arts Work Center in Provincetown, Massachusetts, and has received grants from the National Endowment for the Arts and from the state arts councils of Massachusetts, Illinois, and Vermont. Her essay "Dreaming in Public: A Provincetown Memoir" appeared in *The Best American Essays 1988*. She has taught at Middlebury College and at Northeastern Illinois University and is currently the Mary Blossom Lee Professor of poetry at Florida Atlantic University.

Of "Havana Birth," Mitchell writes: "In an old blues Brownie

McGhee sings, 'If you've got a good girl, don't ever tell your man friends what your good girl can do.' Probably the same reticence should apply to the poet's poem, so in talking about 'Havana Birth,' I shall try not to blab about our deeper intimacies.

"I really did spend an entire winter trying to catch a pigeon on a beach in Florida. I must have been five or six. When I finally caught the bird, I was thrilled, but also terrified—by the reality of the pigeon, by a desire utterly separate from my own, the pigeon's heart pulsing against my fingers, the wings pushing up against my hands. I let the bird go. Through most of my adult life, I was haunted by that experience and kept trying to write about it. It wasn't until I started to think of what at first seemed a very different subject—the number of times we are born in our lives, those experiences so crucial to us that we tumble out of them glistening and wet and new—that I began to think of my catching the pigeon as a birth. With that realization, the first five stanzas came very easily. I knew what my stanzaic unit would be almost at once, something that's important to me since I have to visualize a poem, its masses, its weights and mountains, in order to write it. I also knew early on I would be using rhyme within, rather than at the ends of lines. When I had almost finished the fifth stanza, my writing was interrupted by a phone call. Usually such interruptions have no effect whatsoever on my writing: I simply pick up where I left off. But this time when I returned to my typewriter, I found the poem had sealed itself off, like a vein that shuts down sometimes when you give blood. It wasn't until thirteen months later that I was able to continue the poem. Perhaps the fact that I had left New England for Florida, where the experience with the pigeon had occurred, helped get the poem going again. When it did pick up, the subject had moved out from the personal to include the social and the political. And by then, the poem had also found its own definition of birth, not only as freeing oneself from the mother but more importantly as the struggle to enter the world."

PAUL MONETTE was born in Lawrence, Massachusetts, in 1945 and attended Yale University. He is the author of *Borrowed Time: An AIDS Memoir* (Harcourt Brace Jovanovich, 1988), which was nominated for a National Book Critics Circle Award in biography. His novels include *Afterlife* (Crown, 1990). *Love Alone: 18 Elegies for Rog*, the most recent of his three collections of poetry, was published by St. Martin's Press. He lives in Los Angeles.

LAURA MORIARTY was born in St. Paul, Minnesota, in 1952. She is currently the manager of the American Poetry Archives for the Poetry Center at San Francisco State University. In 1983 she was a co-winner of the Poetry Center Book Award for her book *Persia* (Chance Additions, 1983). Her other books include *Two Cross Seizings* (Sombre Reptiles, 1980), *Duse* (Coincidence Press, 1986), and *like roads* (Kelsey Street Press, 1990). Forthcoming are *La Futura* (Zasterle Press) and *Rondeaux* (Roof Books).

Of "La Malinche," Moriarty writes: "It is complicated for a North American to travel in Mexico. You have the chance to experience your complicity in the history of exchanges between the two United States. Then there are the daily exchanges in which sexual and racial politics are played out. It's not all good news. An intense refrain, something like a lyric, embeds itself in the narrative. One thing—what you are doing and what is being done to you— explains the other. I wanted this relationship of song to story in 'La Malinche' because it seemed like life."

THYLIAS MOSS was born in Cleveland in 1954. She teaches at Phillips Academy in Andover, Massachusetts. *Pyramid of Bone*, her second volume of poems (University of Virginia Press, 1989), was nominated for the National Book Critics Circle Award. She recently received a poetry fellowship from the National Endowment for the Arts, and her work was included in the 1989 edition of *The Best American Poetry*. A new collection, *At Redbone's*, is forthcoming from Cleveland State University Press.

Of "There Will Be Animals," Moss writes: "I am a small woman full of doubts, full because being small means that what might be normal, reasonable quantities and doses for someone else are excesses for me. I fill quickly. Yet there is room for something else: faith in ideals. Not paradise—I don't want or need paradise, because I don't think it will teach us anything but pride (some have too much of that) and haughtiness, belief that what we did was right, that the ultimate good was achieved through what we did, no matter how recklessly performed. No; I mean those other ideals, the 'no man is an island' theory, the idea that no human is complete, self-contained, entirely self-providing, absolved from need altogether. Understand from this that I believe that struggling will in fact change us, that the form of paradise we do eventually have will not be permanent, immutable, or total (a part of existence might become ideal while other parts lag in destitute hellishness— most lagging is a form of poverty). We will have to work at the maintenance of our ideals; the attainable paradise will always be threatened as we work to control and curb (only occasionally successfully) instincts and passions that are part of our design, that therefore must accompany us wherever we go, even to paradise. Recognizing then—and this is easy recognition, for it is how we know ourselves—that we have limitations, that what makes us human, keeps us human, keeps us hungry; we cannot hope to discover the answers by ourselves. But since hunger demands feeding and what we want to be are gluttons, I have every faith that we will seek answers to eat. And they are going to come from the unlikely source, from what we have dominion over—licensed dominion, if one defers to biblical entitlement—from what is below us, inferior, subjugated and all that, because we need humbling first before we can alter our evolution and move toward becoming marvelous beings. The animals, the residents of that parallel world, the one that watches ours, that already realizes it is our teacher since we learned from it the survival tactics of hunt, kill, maim, attack, consume, and destroy, that on our higher human level become systems of cruelty; that world, that natural world can certainly teach us something else just as effectively as it taught us war. Judging from how well we learned that first lesson, who can then doubt that any other lesson would be as perfectly learned, perfectly implemented even into our very definition of ourselves? So, elimination of doubt is what that poem says to me. An insistence on hope despite everything, a belief that hope is rational is what I am trying to prove to myself in that poem, and to anyone else who needs convincing. Accomplishing that, this small woman has room to live."

MELINDA MUELLER's first collection of poetry, *Asleep In Another Country*, was published by Jawbone Press in 1979. It received an award of "Special Distinction" in the Elliston Competition for small-press books the following year. Mueller graduated with a Bachelor of Science degree from the University of Washington. She has been a science teacher in Seattle-area schools for twelve years, and has served on the faculty of several writers' conferences, most recently in Sitka, Alaska. She was a co-author of Washington State's first list of threatened and endangered plant species. In 1979 she received the Washington State Governor's Award for Writing.

Of "Teratology," Mueller writes: "Many of my students write poetry—so did I in high school. I wrote it the same way they do: I waited for an idea to present itself (you know, the moment of inspiration), and then I wrote a poem. I thought that if I worked on writing *before* that illuminating flash, I'd spoil it. The stuff I wrote was dreadful.

"Now the idea I have about writing is the sort you'd expect from a science teacher. I think it's like the old junior high school crystal-growing project. You dissolve sugar or a permanganate—whatever —in warm water until the solution is supersaturated. When the solution cools, you suspend in it a small seed-crystal. If the solution is concentrated enough, a large crystal will grow around the seed —and if not, the seed dissolves. And hasn't everyone read poems whose original insight is dispersed among dilute images?

"Nearly ten years ago, I read an essay about Phineas Gage (his skull, and the tamping iron, are preserved at the Harvard Medical School). I wrote this monologue, and liked it, but it didn't seem to advance beyond good description; not enough on its own for a poem. It went into a file I have called 'Spare Parts.'

"By 1988, the file held—among many other items—an article about the Vatican's conference on Satan, another about Haiti's wrecked 1987 elections, and some notes from firsthand accounts of the Civil War. The line about 'the God who has everything' was there, written in anger after hearing a minister say, at a friend's funeral, 'Our loss is God's gain.' I didn't have it in mind that any of these bits belonged together in a poem.

"One evening I encountered, in an essay by Stephen Jay Gould, the word *teratology*. I looked it up: the study of monsters. That, it turned out, was the seed crystal. The Spare Parts oddments and some unwritten memories, all having to do with a kind of fury, coalesced around it. The poem was written in three days. This is typical of how I write now: by accretion in advance of the unplannable insight."

LAURA MULLEN was born in Los Angeles in 1958 and raised in various parts of California. She received her BA from the University of California, Berkeley, in 1984 and her MFA from the University of Iowa in 1985. She has been the recipient of *Ironwood*'s Stanford Prize, a grant from the Whiting Foundation, and a National Endowment for the Arts Fellowship. During 1989–90 she was a Visiting Assistant Professor in creative writing and American studies at Colby College in Maine.

Of "They," Mullen writes: "I was living in a boardinghouse in Iowa City and struggling, as always, with the desire for perfection that constantly threatens to shut me up. Under the pressures of graduate school, I was learning to get around it by simply forcing myself to write, just write. It was near the end of the summer— the evenings were still very long—and I came home and, not, of course, really wanting to sit down with the blank paper and possible failure, tried to call my friend Joseph Lease, because he had once accused me of liking my 'beauty straight up,' and I was coming to realize what the problem with that might be. So there was this tension (and luckily Joseph wasn't home) which I was beginning to feel between my desire to be perfect and beautiful and in the world of Art (which seemed safe but was, by itself, getting a little deadly) and my desire to live and to speak. And it seemed that if I was really going to go on as a writer I was going to have to find a way to let life in, 'real life,' in all its ugliness and chaos—because I was very frightened, and that was how 'life' appeared to me. It's only from this distance that I've realized that the way in which I found to try to hold it all together while also letting go of it (trying to make it both secure and free) was informed by the jazz I grew up hearing—the Coltrane, for instance, of 'My Favorite Things.' You establish the 'like,' pull it out to where resemblance and coherence disappear, and then, out of apparent chaos, bring back order in a way that seems to prove it was there all along. But there's something sad about it, that's what I was feeling then, and that's in the poem, something sad about the place that the need for control and safety gets you back to, leaves you in. . . . I don't even like 'My Favorite Things.' "

ALICE NOTLEY lives in New York City. Her most recent book is *At Night the States* (Yellow Press, 1987). She received a fellowship from the National Endowment for the Arts in 1980, a General Electric Foundation Award in 1984, and awards from the Fund for Poetry in 1987 and 1989. She edited Ted Berrigan's *A Certain Slant of Sunlight* for O Books.

Of "(2 pages from a long poem in progress)," Notley writes: "These pages are excerpted from a long poem I'm still working on. They are representative of how the poem looks, & of its measure. The first two sections of the poem are made up of individual dreamlike stories or episodes—like these; the third contains a more continuous narrative; & the fourth, & last, I'm beginning now (January 1990). Most of the poem takes place underground."

MICHAEL PALMER was born in New York City in 1943. He has lived in San Francisco since 1969. He is the author of six collections of poetry, the two most recent being *First Figure* (1984) and *Sun* (1988), both from North Point Press. *Sun* received the PEN West poetry award. He has taught at Harvard, Berkeley, New College of California, and the University of California at San Diego. He is currently a Guggenheim Fellow in poetry.

Of "Six Hermetic Songs," Palmer writes: "The *Corpus Hermeticum* formed a part of the vast 'poetic lore' as conceived by the poet Robert Duncan. The veiled speech of these 'songs' (in a loose sense) is meant as a kind of homage to Duncan and his poetic practice, echoing fragments of our conversations over many years concerning measure, the body, and the dance. At points the sequence also echoes the Italian *poeti ermetici* of this century. Late in the composition of these poems, on an island off the coast of Massachusetts, I came across a turn-of-the-century copy of *The Egyptian Book of the Dead*, which appears in the epigraph and in the two final poems."

ROBERT PINSKY was born in Long Branch, New Jersey, in 1940. After many years in Berkeley, California, he now teaches in the graduate creative writing program at Boston University. "Pilgrimage" appears in his fourth book of poems, *The Want Bone* (Ecco Press, 1990). His previous book, *History of My Heart*, was awarded the William Carlos Williams Prize by the Poetry Society of America.

Pinsky writes: "The virtually sexual intensity of language and feeling in Psalm 139—the Hebrew poet's attempt to approach the absolute—inspired some of the phrases and setting in 'Pilgrimage.' I'll try to say a little, not about the poem's meaning, but about the thinking and feeling behind it.

"The poem tries to imagine something like the early days of Judaism in a setting something like the Yosemite Falls of California. A paradigm, but with specific textures. The goal is less a conception of worship—far less any specific mode of worship—than a conception of passion in a place among a people. The ritual conceives an Absolute, but exactly because it is *conceived*, the Absolute is always changing and flowing like the falls or a sentence in a poem, something is always next or behind. Always near the peak, always on the way to it, always not at it.

"Religion concerns me in *The Want Bone* not quite exactly in itself but as a vivid, charged example of the passion to create. Making rituals, making buildings, making names, making chants of like sounds, making music—all, in this context, make up the communal expression of what is sometimes called making love. Arousal flies up above a consciousness that this ardent making, in its deadly struggle with the imperfection of what was, may also twist into a passionate destroying: pogroms, extermination of American Indian civilizations, etc."

JENDI REITER was born in New York City in 1972. She is currently a first-year student at Barnard College, majoring in biology. She won the 1988 Elias Lieberman Student Poetry Award from the Poetry Society of America. In 1989 she received a Younger Scholars Grant from the National Endowment for the Humanities to write a thesis on T. S. Eliot's *Four Quartets*. "Service Includes Free Lifetime Updating" was written in the fall term of her senior year in high school.

Reiter writes: "My aim in this poem was to show how the forgotten power of ideals eventually overtakes a culture that has cynically preserved the images and rhetoric of the ideals while using them to promote their opposites or banal concerns. An instance of this is the episode with 'one of Ayn Rand's minor characters,' which came from a story a girl told me about a summer camp where they had turned one of Rand's novels into a play. The novel, *Anthem*, originally promotes Rand's ideals of individualism and human dignity; however, at the end of the play, the campers had the hero and heroine go to sleep and dream about how awful the world would be if those ideals were realized. The worst part of the episode was, for me, the utter indifference with which the scriptwriters had assumed the right to use someone else's words to attack her own ideals. My title is a line from an ad for a résumé service. When I first read it, it gave me a sense that something meaningful had been reduced to something glib and mundane, as if one's life, and not just one's résumé, could be brought up to date by a résumé service. The fact that no such promise was intended indicated how cheap and powerless the idea of 'lifetime' has become. However, when something powerful starts to interpret literally the words that had been pronounced cynically, a reckoning begins to happen, not with anger but with the inexorable, even patient deliberateness of logic."

JOAN RETALLACK was born in the pre-postmodern era in New York City. She is on the faculties of the Honors Program at the University of Maryland and the Institute for Writing and Thinking at Bard College. In 1985 she won a Pushcart Prize and her volume of poetry, *Circumstantial Evidence*, was published by S.O.S. Press. She is currently at work on a book-length, mixed-genre manuscript, and on a long poem called "WESTERN CIV." She lives in Chevy Chase, Maryland.

Of "JAPANESE PRESENTATION, I & II," Retallack writes:

"• I don't claim this poem as a scene of ritual self-sacrifice, and yet it is about edges.

• Even Mallarmé wrote, 'Every Thought emits a Throw of the Dice.'

• If sex takes place most abundantly in ellipsis, art and the rest of life charge one another in the gaps that edges (in the edges that gaps) reveal.

• Transgressing one margin for another, they experienced their fear as a form of love.
• The word is the edge of a Figure-Ground shifting in its articulation."

DONALD REVELL was born in New York City in 1954. An associate professor at the University of Denver, he has won a National Poetry Series Prize, a Pushcart Prize, and a fellowship from the National Endowment for the Arts. His books of verse are *From the Abandoned Cities* (Harper & Row, 1983), *The Gaza of Winter* (University of Georgia Press, 1988), and *New Dark Ages* (Wesleyan University Press, 1990). His work was included in the 1988 edition of *The Best American Poetry*.

Revell writes: " 'The Old Causes' is, in its way, a meditation on the role of tyranny in personal life. For a long time, I have been obsessed with George Orwell's saying that 'the literature of the twentieth century will be the literature of totalitarianism.' Believing him implicitly, yet without ever being wholly certain of Orwell's exact intention, I have looked for ways of writing to the subject of tyranny without collaboration or self-praise (the Scylla and Charybdis of political writing). I have come to think of our century as a period of many contiguous, occasionally overlapping totalitarianisms: some overt, some subtle. In 'The Old Causes,' I try to summon images of conventional modern tyranny: the AIDS epidemic that has invaded and distorted all intimacy to such an extent that it might almost be valid to say, 'We shall not love with our bodies again.' "

ADRIENNE RICH was born in Baltimore, Maryland, in 1929. She is the author of many volumes of poetry, including *The Fact of a Doorframe: Poems Selected and New* (1984), *Your Native Land, Your Life* (1986), and *Time's Power* (1989), all from Norton. She has published three prose books: *Of Woman Born: Motherhood as Experience and Institution* (1976; new ed., 1986); *On Lies, Secrets and Silence* (1979); and *Blood, Bread and Poetry* (1986), also from Norton. She was the first recipient of the Ruth Lilly Prize for outstanding achievement in American poetry. She has received the Brandeis Creative Arts Commission Medal for Poetry, the Elmer Holmes Bobst Award in Poetry from New York University, and the Fund for Human Dignity Award from the National Gay Task Force. She is an active member of New Jewish Agenda, a national organization of progressive Jews, and is a founding editor of the Jewish feminist journal *Bridges*. She teaches English and feminist studies at Stanford University.

Of "Living Memory," Rich writes: "I hope that the poem speaks for itself. Readers might like to know that the 'tall, gaunt woman' was Eleanor Roosevelt, that the statue 'Grief' was commissioned by Henry Adams from the sculptor Saint-Gaudens in memory of his wife, Clover Adams (Marion Hooper), who, a talented photographer, had committed suicide by drinking photographic chemicals."

MICHAEL RYAN was born in St. Louis in 1946. He has published three volumes of poetry: *Threats Instead of Trees* (Yale University Press, 1974), *In Winter* (Holt, 1981), and *God Hunger* (Viking, 1989). A collection of his essays titled *On the Nature of Poetry* is forthcoming from Viking. His awards include a Whiting Writers Award, a Guggenheim Fellowship, the Yale Series of Younger Poets Award, a National Book Award nomination, and two fellowships from the National Endowment for the Arts. He teaches in the MFA Program for Writers at Warren Wilson College.

Of "Switchblade," Ryan writes: "We tell one another hundreds of stories every day, some more important than others. I'm very interested in how they're shaped, what they do, and why we need them. 'Switchblade' tells part of a story that's important to me, but if it has any significance beyond that it's because of its music: the moment-to-moment manifold relationships of stress, phrasing, and varieties of rhyme to one another and to the syntax of the sentences and to their meaning. I think the most articulate thing you can say about a poem is the way that you read it, and I write my poems to be experienced, to be voiced and heard, so I hope anyone who likes 'Switchblade' will read it aloud."

DAVID ST. JOHN was born in Fresno, California, in 1949. He is the author of three collections of poetry: *Hush* (1976), *The Shore* (1980), and *No Heaven* (1985), all from Houghton Mifflin. A recipient of fellowships from the National Endowment for the Arts, the Guggenheim Foundation, and the Ingram Merrill Foundation, he is poetry editor of *The Antioch Review* and a professor of English at the University of Southern California.

St. John writes: "While living in Italy in 1984–85, I began a sequence of poems that use Italian backdrops; these poems form a kind of poetic sketchbook, and several are situated in Rome, where I was living at the time. One of my favorite cafés in Rome was and is the one mentioned in 'Last Night with Rafaella,' a place called Rosati just at the edge of the Piazza del Popolo. It was once a particularly glamorous place, especially popular with Roman writers and movie folks in the '60s (Charles Wright tells me he used to see Michelangelo Antonioni and Monica Vitti there), and it still draws its share of familiar faces. While sitting at one of its outside tables, one could watch not only the flow of Roman life through the Piazza del Popolo but the more intimate dramas enacted at the neighboring tables. In my brief prose piece 'Roman Noon,' I recall watching the almost operatic arrival of an elegant Roman woman who had come to meet her lover at Rosati; it was while eavesdropping on this couple and others like them that the idea for a more lighthearted Roman poem began to form. I didn't write the poem until I'd returned to the States, in fact not until the fall of 1986 when I came across some notes sketched out at Rosati. It took me almost another year and a half to complete the poem in its present version, which stands as testimony, I hope, in praise of Roman life, humor, and, most certainly, Rafaella."

JAMES SCHUYLER was born in Chicago in 1923. His books of poetry include *Freely Espousing* (Doubleday, 1969), *The Crystal Lithium* (Random House, 1972), *Hymn to Life* (Random House, 1974), *The Morning of the Poem* (Farrar, Straus & Giroux, 1980), and *A Few Days* (Random House, 1985). *The Morning of the Poem* won the Pulitzer Prize. He has also published three novels, one of them written in collaboration with John Ashbery. James Schuyler's *Selected Poems* was published in 1988 by Farrar, Straus & Giroux. He lives in New York City.

Schuyler writes: " 'Haze' was written one humid August afternoon in the guest house at Little Portion, an Episcopal Franciscan Friary on the North Shore of Long Island, not far from Port Jefferson. Like many other of my poems, this is about what can be seen out the window: except here, though nothing is said about it, the poem combines the view from two windows, and several times of day. I do not usually take such license."

FREDERICK SEIDEL was born in St. Louis in 1936, attended Harvard College, and now lives in New York City. In 1980 his book *Sunrise* won the National Book Critics Circle Award for poetry. Knopf published his *Poems, 1959–1979* and a new collection, *These Days,* in 1989.

CHARLES SIMIC was born in Yugoslavia in 1938. He was educated at the University of Chicago and at New York University. His recent books include *Unending Blues* (1986), *The World Doesn't End* (1989), and *The Book of Gods and Devils* (1990), all from Harcourt Brace Jovanovich. In 1990 he received the Pulitzer Prize for poetry. He teaches at the University of New Hampshire.

Of "The Initiate," Simic writes: "The young man in the poem has been reading the great mystics night and day. He dreams of being initiated into the mysteries. In the meantime, he's poor, unemployed, and a stranger in New York City. He walks around expecting a miracle to happen."

GUSTAF SOBIN was born in Boston in 1935. After completing his studies (Choate School, 1953; Brown University, 1958) he moved to Provence and has lived there ever since. His books of poetry are *Wind Chrysalid's Rattle* (1980) and *Celebration of the Sound Through* (1982), both from Montemora, and *The Earth as Air* (1984) and *Voyaging Portraits* (1989), from New Directions. A novel, *Venus Blue,* will be published by Bloomsbury (London) in 1991.

Sobin writes: "One fragment, it would seem, invites another. Rather than closing autonomously upon itself (such as with the 'well-rounded statement') each fragment—each viable fragment, that is—as if powered by its own incompleteness, begs its own suite, sequence, eventual incorporation. By placing, replacing, displacing one fragment after another, 'Transparent Itineraries' proceeds by deliberately orchestrated segments, breath-scraps, linguistic 'remainders.' Each entry, ideally, would both signify *something* and suggest, by implication, its own successor: i.e., *something else, something further*. Thus, the 'itinerary.' These 'itineraries,' in themselves, offer no destination. They are a measure, however, of the very distances that they take and, in their own unravelling, of whatever landscapes, *en route*, that they might happen to reveal."

ELIZABETH SPIRES was born in Lancaster, Ohio, in 1952. Her books of poems are *Globe* (Wesleyan University Press, 1981), *Swan's Island* (Holt, 1985), and *Annonciade* (Viking Penguin, 1989). Currently she lives in Baltimore and teaches in the writing seminars at Johns Hopkins and at Goucher College. Her work was included in the 1989 edition of *The Best American Poetry*.

Spires writes: " 'Primos' was written after a visit to the Isles of Scilly, twenty-eight miles off Land's End, England. The figurehead is on display in the Tresco Abbey Gardens, part of a collection of twenty-eight shipwrecked figureheads from nineteenth-century merchant vessels that was assembled, starting around 1840, by Augustus Smith, 'Lord Proprietor' of the Islands. A booklet published by the British National Maritime Museum gives the following account of the Spanish barque *Primos*, shipwrecked in 1871 on the Seven Stones: 'In heavy weather and about dawn, she hit these notorious rocks between the Islands and Land's End. . . . All eleven crew were drowned except for Vincenzo Defilice who had a remarkable escape. After swimming for some hours he found a floating hen coop, onto which he climbed and kept afloat for a further hour. He then saw the ship's figurehead, to which he was able to cling for several hours before one of the *Primos'* own boats drifted by; in this he rowed himself to English Island Neck where he was rescued by Scilly pilots. By these strange methods he had travelled a distance of at least 8½ miles in the open sea. According to tradition, Defilice knew he would be saved because of the serene expression on the face of the figurehead.' (From the booklet *'Valhalla': The Tresco Ships' Figurehead Collection.*)"

GERALD STERN was born in Pittsburgh in 1925. His newest book is *Leaving Another Kingdom: Selected Poems* (Harper & Row, 1990). He has won a Guggenheim Fellowship, three grants from the NEA, the Lamont Prize for *Lucky Life* (1977), and the Melville Cane

Award for *The Red Coal* (1981). He makes his home in Iowa and Pennsylvania, and is on the faculty of the Writers' Workshop at the University of Iowa.

Stern writes: " 'Saving My Skin from Burning' is a poem that was locked inside another poem, like the proverbial Chinese boxes, or Ukrainian eggs, or Russian dolls. I was writing a spring—a rebirth—poem in the late winter of 1988 that was the result, as far as subject matter was concerned, of the long walks I was taking then along three or four gorgeous roads in the mountainous out-reaches of Perry County in central Pennsylvania. I remember I was walking up to three hours at a stretch and I was always in a state of elation during my walks. It was the first spring, the false one, marked by a little mud and some mad watercress and one or two berserk birds that we get almost every year at that time in central and eastern Pennsylvania. For whatever reason, I was thinking of the prophet Jeremiah in connection with the (false) spring. I think it was because I had discovered a kind of tunnel, where the water flowed in, under a roof of grass and ice and frozen leaves, and a pit of mud at the end of that tunnel that reminded me of the pit— or dungeon—where Jeremiah was imprisoned, because of his vile tongue. Though there had to be another reason I was thinking of Jeremiah; maybe it was living among the Babylonians. I thought of him lying in the mud and screaming for help. And I thought of the rags and clouts and ropes that Ebedmelech the Ethiopian let down to him (38:11), and of the mire that was mentioned in the Scriptures (38:6) that Jeremiah had 'sunk into.' My original title for the poem was 'Jeremiah Bringing in the Spring.'

"As it often happens, I was struck, after a little while, with the mannered quality of the poem. I wasn't *being myself* or *speaking in my own voice*. That's the way I put it. And I realized that the true center of the poem was Jeremiah's terrifying experience and not the long preparation, consisting mostly of elegant nature descrip-tion, that preceded it in the first version. Also, I either read some-where, or I imagined, that the pit or dungeon that Jeremiah was thrown into was actually a cistern, and I immediately made a con-nection with the huge abandoned cistern in the backyard of my former house in Raubsville, Pennsylvania, along the Delaware, and even described it in part in the second version of the poem. For example, there *were* ledges inside that cistern, and there *was* a pipe, and there was a manhole in the center of the roof, the actual entrance. I had great plans for that cistern once. It was going to be a meditation room, a music room, a place of absolute silence. It was—to my memory—a twelve-foot cube.

"I don't have much to say about the 'meaning' or psychic significance of the poem, as it now stands. I know I was finally able to write it in a minute or two. Of course, it is an 'escape' poem and a 'rebirth' poem, and has connections with dozens of myths and memories. I am surprised, as I think of it now, why more attention hasn't been paid to the hidden meaning of the event. Perhaps because it was done so literally and with no allusion at all to anything mythological or magical. I must confess, also, that, as I wrote it, my mind was only on the cistern and my imprisonment (and liberation) and Jeremiah's. I had no thoughts of those other things. If the poem succeeds and has richness and resonance it is for that reason."

MARK STRAND was born in Summerside, Prince Edward Island, in 1934. He is a professor at the University of Utah and holds a John D. and Catherine T. MacArthur Foundation Fellowship. His book of poems *The Continuous Life* is being published in 1990 by Knopf. He was recently named Poet Laureate of the United States.

Of "Orpheus Alone," Strand writes: "Since the myth of Orpheus is the central myth of poetic creation, I wanted to write an Orphic poem. But I didn't want to dwell on the relationship of Orpheus and Eurydice or on the moment of their final separation when Orpheus looks back and Eurydice returns to Hades. I wanted to write a poem on the sources of poetry. And I wanted it to be as lavish a poem as I could write. I drew inspiration from other poems about Orpheus—not just from Ovid's, or Virgil's in the fourth Georgic, but from Rilke's, especially in Rika Lesser's translation, and from one stanza in particular, the one that begins 'So beloved / that from one lyre / more mourning came,' and in recent poetry from John Ashbery's great and original 'Syringa' and Jorie Graham's brilliant 'Orpheus and Eurydice.' "

JAMES TATE was born in Kansas City, Missouri, in 1943. He was awarded the Yale Younger Poets Prize in 1966. His most recent books of poetry are *Constant Defender* (Ecco Press, 1983) and *Reckoner* (Wesleyan University Press, 1986). "Distance from Loved Ones" is the title poem of a new collection. He teaches at the University of Massachusetts.

SIDNEY WADE was born in Englewood, New Jersey, in 1951. She currently teaches American and British literature at Istanbul University, on a Fulbright Fellowship. Her first book of poems, *Empty Sleeves*, will be published by the University of Georgia Press in the winter of 1991.

Of "Aurora Borealis and the Body Louse," Wade writes: "I had thought, enchanted by Wallace Stevens's poem's title, 'Saint John and the Back-Ache,' that I had simply tried to find as comically incongruous a pair of characters and then write a poem in their voices. Now, however, rereading Stevens's piece, I find to my surprise I seem to have retained more than a little of its substance. I did, however, rework it in the light of my own 'little ignorance,' which, as Stevens says, is everything."

ROSANNA WARREN was born in Fairfield, Connecticut, in 1953. She is currently an assistant professor in the departments of English and modern languages and in the University Professors Program at Boston University. She has received a grant from the Ingram Merrill Foundation and a Guggenheim Fellowship. Her books of poetry include *Snow Day* (Palaemon Press, 1981) and *Each Leaf Shines Separate* (Norton, 1984). She is the editor of *The Art of Translation* (Northeastern University Press, 1989) and is the poetry consultant for *Partisan Review*.

Of "The Cormorant," Warren writes: "It's difficult, and possibly superfluous, for the poet to comment on a poem that's found at least its provisional form. After all, one wrestled the thing out of the 'comment' stage into rhymed quatrains, in this case, and made them as tight as possible. . . . The problems with this poem involved the multiple perspectives of narrator, husband/father, children, and the overelaborate economic metaphors. The poem grew from the perception of the contrast between the somber 'deacon spruces' and the riotous yellow hawkweed on an island in Maine, a perception that grew intrinsicate with the surprise and sorrow I felt at the death of a beloved aunt, far away. The tight stanzas, I suppose, were an attempt to 'hold' her: an impossible attempt, in any event."

RICHARD WILBUR was born in New York City in 1921. His *New and Collected Poems*, published by Harcourt Brace Jovanovich in 1988, won the *Los Angeles Times* Poetry Award and the Pulitzer Prize. In 1987–88 he served as the nation's second official poet laureate, succeeding Robert Penn Warren.

Of "A Wall in the Woods: Cummington," Wilbur writes: "This poem is in two voices, the second opposing whatever there is of elegiac sadness in the first. I suppose that 'A Wall in the Woods' may raise the technical question of whether a two-part poem can effectively shift from blank verse to syllabics. But perhaps not: the rhythms of part 2 are apparently strong enough to have disguised, for some good readers, the 5775 syllabic pattern which I used in hopes of embodying the fluent skittering of the chipmunk. Yes, it is a chipmunk. Two of my correspondents, neither a New Englander, took it to be a bird; but it seems to me that I give sufficient evidence for its being *Tamias striatus*. In any case, there's a certain additional immediacy to be got by not naming what you are talking about."

ELEANOR WILNER was born in Ohio in 1937. Her books include *Sarah's Choice* (1989) and *Shekhinah* (1984), both from the Phoenix Poets Series of the University of Chicago Press; *maya*, the 1979 Juniper Prize volume from the University of Massachusetts Press; and a book on visionary imagination, *Gathering the Winds* (Johns Hopkins, 1975). *Sarah's Choice* was nominated for a *Los Angeles Times* Book Prize. She is currently on the faculty of the MFA Writing Program of Warren Wilson College, visiting poet at the University of Chicago, and an associate editor of *Calyx*.

Of "Reading the Bible Backwards," Wilner writes: "The poem's occasion is little more than that—a door blown open by the wind. A line from Thomas Lovell Beddoes: 'How thou art like the daisy in Noah's meadow, / On which the foremost drop of rain fell warm / And soft at evening.'

"The poem merely records what the mind's eye saw. Its dissolution of old forms is felt, somehow, as restorative, as if it were part of an act of the changing of cultural memory, freeing us from our own mad anthropocentrism, an act so collective and so ineluctable that each poet, each poem, that carries it is no more than a drop in a universal flood.

"Its details matter. Each, like our cells, carries a history: the altar whose spilled blood invites the rain, the angels with 'oiled flesh' and 'smoldering swords,' the child 'bright . . . as a lemon,' the bitter smell of 'wet swaddling clothes,' the 'liquid tongue' of lullaby, the 'old kings uncrowned,' the curtain on the 'lit tableau,' the sea-softened features of the gorgon, the 'shy tangles' of giant squid, the unraveling 'in filaments of straw' of the basket that carried the man-as-god.

"This is not the destructive flood of the Bible; water, here, is not a weapon. It is a medium of change that carries its own forms, those angels of the deep, within it. So this is a poem of the end, not of the world, but of its opposite: the end of teleology, the end of a sublime presumption."

CHARLES WRIGHT was born in Pickwick Dam, Tennessee, in 1935. He lives in Charlottesville, Virginia, and teaches in the English department of the University of Virginia. His most recent book of poems is *Zone Journals* (Farrar, Straus & Giroux, 1988); his prose book, *Halflife*, was published by the University of Michigan Press in 1988. In 1990 Farrar, Straus & Giroux will publish *The World of the 10,000 Things: Poems 1980–1990*. He was a co-recipient of the 1983 American Book Award in poetry for his *Country Music: Selected Early Poems* (Wesleyan University Press).

Wright writes: " 'Saturday Morning Journal' is one of fifteen 'apocryphal' journals that are collected under the heading *Xionia* and are adjunct to the book *Zone Journals*. Shorter for the most part, more fragmentary but more strongly centered, they attempt to fill in the doctrinal gaps and lapses of the larger whole. 'Saturday Morning Journal' speaks to its ultimate failure of design and the overwhelming problem of inarticulation."

MAGAZINES WHERE THE POEMS
WERE FIRST PUBLISHED

American Poetry Review, eds. Stephen Berg, David Bonanno, and Arthur Vogelsang. 1704 Walnut Street, Philadelphia, Pa. 19103.

Antæus, ed. Daniel Halpern. The Ecco Press, 26 West 17th Street, New York, N.Y. 10011.

The Atlantic Monthly, poetry ed. Peter Davison. 8 Arlington Street, Boston, Mass. 02116.

Avec, ed. Cydney Chadwick. P.O. Box 1059, Penngrove, Calif. 94951.

Black Warrior Review, eds. Jeff Mock (vol. 15) and Mark Dawson (vol. 16). P.O. Box 2936, Tuscaloosa, Ala. 35487-2936.

Boulevard, ed. Richard Burgin. 2400 Chestnut Street, #3301, Philadelphia, Pa. 19103.

Broadway, eds. James Schuyler and Charles North. Hanging Loose Press, 231 Wyckoff Street, Brooklyn, N.Y. 11217.

Denver Quarterly, ed. Donald Revell. University of Denver, Denver, Colo. 80208.

Fine Madness, eds. Sean Bentley, Louis Bergsagel, Christine Deavel, John Malek, and John Marshall. P.O. Box 15176, Seattle, Wash. 98115-0176.

The Gettysburg Review, ed. Peter Stitt. Gettysburg College, Gettysburg, Pa. 17325.

Grand Street, ed. Jean Stein. 135 Central Park West, New York, N.Y. 10023.

Hambone, ed. Nathaniel Mackey. 134 Hunolt Street, Santa Cruz, Calif. 95060.

Hanging Loose, eds. Robert Hershon, Dick Lourie, Mark Pawlak, and Ron Schreiber. 231 Wyckoff Street, Brooklyn, N.Y. 11217.

Harvard Magazine, poetry ed. Donald Hall. 7 Ware Street, Cambridge, Mass. 02138.

How(ever), eds. Meredith Stricker and Myung Mi Kim. 1171 East Jefferson, Iowa City, Iowa 52245.

The Hudson Review, eds. Paula Deitz and Frederick Morgan. 684 Park Avenue, New York, N.Y. 10021.

The Iowa Review, ed. David Hamilton. 308 EPB, University of Iowa, Iowa City, Iowa 52242.

Michigan Quarterly Review, ed. Laurence Goldstein. University of Michigan, 3032 Rackham Building, Ann Arbor, Mich. 48109-1070.

The Nation, poetry ed. Grace Schulman. 72 Fifth Avenue, New York, N.Y. 10011.

New Letters, ed. James McKinley. 109 Scofield Hall, University of Missouri/Kansas City, 5100 Rockhill Road, Kansas City, Mo. 64110.

The New Republic, poetry ed. Richard Howard. 1220 19th Street, NW, Washington, D.C. 20036.

The New Yorker, poetry ed. Alice Quinn. 25 West 43rd Street, New York, N.Y. 10036.

O.blek, eds. Peter Gizzi and Connell McGrath. Box 836, Stockbridge, Mass. 01262.

Ontario Review, ed. Raymond Smith. 9 Honey Brook Drive, Princeton, N.J. 08540.

The Paris Review, poetry ed. Patricia Storace. 541 East 72nd Street, New York, N.Y. 10021.

Ploughshares, ed. DeWitt Henry. Emerson College, 100 Beacon Street, Boston, Mass. 02116.

The Sewanee Review, ed. George Core. University of the South, Sewanee, Tenn. 37375.

Southwest Review, ed. Willard Spiegelman. 6410 Airline Road, Southern Methodist University, Dallas, Tex. 75275.

Sulfur, ed. Clayton Eshleman. English Department, Eastern Michigan University, Ypsilanti, Mich. 48197.

Temblor, ed. Leland Hickman. 4624 Cahuenga Blvd., #307, North Hollywood, Calif. 91602.

The Threepenny Review, ed. Wendy Lesser. P.O. Box 9131, Berkeley, Calif. 94709.

Virginia Quarterly Review, poetry ed. Gregory Orr. One West Range, Charlottesville, Va. 22903.

Western Humanities Review, eds. Barry Weller and Charles Berger. 341 Orson Spenser Hall, University of Utah, Salt Lake City, Utah 84112.

The Yale Review, poetry ed. J. D. McClatchy. P.O. Box 1902A Yale Station, New Haven, Conn. 06520.

ACKNOWLEDGMENTS

Grateful acknowledgment is made to the publications from which the poems in this volume were chosen. Unless specifically noted otherwise, copyright of the poems is held by the individual poets.

A. R. Ammons: "The Damned" appeared in *The Yale Review*. Reprinted by permission of the poet.

John Ash: "The Sweeping Gesture" appeared in *Broadway*. Reprinted by permission of the poet and of Hanging Loose Press.

John Ashbery: "Notes from the Air" appeared originally in *The New Yorker*, October 30, 1989. Reprinted by permission; copyright © 1989 John Ashbery.

Marvin Bell: "Victim of Himself" first appeared in *The Atlantic Monthly*. Reprinted by permission of the poet.

Stephen Berg: "First Song/Bankei/1653/" appeared in *The Denver Quarterly*. Reprinted by permission of the poet and the editor of *The Denver Quarterly*.

Mei-mei Berssenbrugge: "Jealousy" from *Empathy* by Mei-mei Berssenbrugge (Station Hill Press). Reprinted by permission of the poet.

Hayden Carruth: "Crucifixion" appeared in *American Poetry Review*. Reprinted by permission of the poet and the editor of *American Poetry Review*.

Anne Carson: "The Life of Towns" was published first in *Grand Street*. Reprinted by permission of the poet and the editor of *Grand Street*.

Raymond Carver: "Wake Up" from *A New Path to the Waterfall* by Raymond Carver, copyright © 1989 by the estate of Raymond Carver. Used by permission of Atlantic Monthly Press. Tess Gallagher's comments appear by her kind permission. "Wake Up" was published in both *Michigan Quarterly Review* and *Poetry*.

Amy Clampitt: "My Cousin Muriel" appeared originally in *The New Yorker*, February 20, 1989. Reprinted by permission; copyright © 1989 Amy Clampitt.

Killarney Clary: "Boys on Street Corners in Santa Ana . . ." from *Who Whispered Near Me* by Killarney Clary. Copyright © 1989 by Killarney Clary. Reprinted by permission of Farrar, Straus & Giroux, Inc.

Robert Creeley: "Thinking" from *Windows* by Robert Creeley. Copyright © 1990 by Robert Creeley. Reprinted by permission of New Directions Publishing Corporation.

Christopher Davis: "Dying in Your Garden of Death to Go Back into My Garden" from *The Tyrant of the Past and the Slave of the Future* by

281